MERRILL
JOHN

MEDIA, MISSION
AND MORALITY

A Scholarly Milestone Essay in Mass Communication
Volume 1

OTHER BOOKS OF INTEREST FROM MARQUETTE BOOKS

Jami Fullerton and Alice Kendrick, *Advertising's War on Terrorism: The Story of the U.S. State Department's Shared Values Initiative* (2006). ISBN: 0-922993-43-2 (cloth); 0-922993-44-0 (paperback)

Mitchell Land and Bill W. Hornaday, *Contemporary Media Ethics: A Practical Guide for Students, Scholars and Professionals* (2006). ISBN: 0-922993-41-6 (cloth); 0-922993-42-4 (paperback)

Stephen D. Cooper, *Watching the Watchdog: Bloggers as the Fifth Estate* (2006). ISBN: 0-922993-46-7 (cloth); 0-922993-47-5 (paperback)

Joey Reagan, *Applied Research Methods for Mass Communicators* (2006). ISBN: 0-922993-45-9 (paperback)

Ralph D. Berenger (ed.), *Cybermedia Go to War: Role of Alternative Media During the 2003 Iraq War* (2006). ISBN: 0-922993-48-3 (cloth); 0-922993-40-1 (paperback)

David Demers, *Dictionary of Mass Communication: A Guide for Students, Scholars and Professionals* (2005). ISBN: 0-922993-35-1 (cloth); 0-922993-25-4 (paperback)

John C. Merrill, Ralph D. Berenger and Charles J. Merrill, *Media Musings: Interviews with Great Thinkers* (2004). ISBN: 0-922993-15-7 (papeback)

Ralph D. Berenger (ed.), *Global Media Go to War: Role of Entertainment and News During the 2003 Iraq War* (2004). ISBN: 0-922993-10-6 (paperback)

Melvin L. DeFleur and Margaret H. DeFleur, *Learning to Hate Americans: How U.S. Media Shape Negative Attitudes Among Teenagers in Twelve Countries* (2003). ISBN: 0-922993-05-X

David Demers (ed.), *Terrorism, Globalization and Mass Communication: Papers Presented at the 2002 Center for Global Media Studies Conference* (2003). ISBN: 0-922993-04-1 (paperback)

MERRILL

JOHN

Calhoun

MEDIA, MISSION
AND MORALITY

A Scholarly Milestone Essay in Mass Communication
Volume I

MARQUETTE BOOKS
Spokane, Washington

70068752   1-10-08

Printed in the United States of America

ABOUT THIS SERIES

The Scholarly Milestone Essays in Mass Communication give leading scholars in the field an opportunity to comment on the major issues facing mass communicators and mass media scholars. The series is by invitation only. Contact Marquette Books at the address below for more information.

Library of Congress Cataloging-in-Publication Data

Merrill, John Calhoun, 1924-
Media, mission, and morality : a scholarly milestone essay in mass communication / John C. Merrill.
p. cm. -- (The scholarly milestone essays in mass communication ; v. 1.)
Includes bibliographical references and index.
ISBN-13: 978-0-922993-59-8 (pbk. : alk. paper)
ISBN-10: 0-922993-59-9 (pbk. : alk. paper)
1. Mass media--Moral and ethical aspects. I. Title.
P94.M47 2006
175--dc22
2006018883

Marquette Books
3107 East 62nd Avenue
Spokane, Washington 99223
509-443-7057 (voice) / 509-448-2191 (fax)
books@marquettebooks.com / www.MarquetteBooks.com

FRONTISPIECE

What has not been examined impartially has not been well examined. Skepticism is therefore the first step toward truth. —*Denis Diderot*

Outside, among your fellows, among strangers, you must preserve appearances, a hundred things you cannot do; but inside, the terrible freedom.
—*Ralph Waldo Emerson*

It is easy to perform a good action, but not easy to acquire a settled habit of performing such actions.
—*Aristotle*

It [the press] is a mass of trivialities and puerilities ... . What is missing is everything worth knowing ... . It is this vast and militant ignorance, this widespread and fathomless prejudice against intelligence, that makes American journalism so pathetically feeble and vulgar, and so generally disreputable.
—*H. L. Mencken*

The voice of the press, so far as by a drift toward monopoly it tends to become exclusive in its wisdom and observation, deprives other voices of a hearing and the public of their contribution. Freedom of the press for the coming period can only continue as an accountable freedom.
—*Commission on Freedom of the Press*

CONTENTS

PREFACE

This essay synthesizes several controversial areas of communications studies, especially as they relate to journalism. It draws heavily on psychology, sociology and especially philosophy, and attempts to cross-pollinate theoretical concepts with practicalities in everyday communication. Philosophical areas of special consideration include epistemology, political philosophy and ethics, with some attention to language philosophy.

For more than 50 years I have added to the literature of journalism and subtracted from the pine forests. This little volume is perhaps my last attempt to summarize some of my ideas and opinions about the public media and to throw out a few new ones. Writing has kept my mind active and, I hope, creative, and my teaching has been a constant pleasure. What fun it is to trudge through the hazy swamps of communication where semantic fog hangs low over the intellectual landscape.

In this diversified field, unsubstantiated assertions and assumptions abound, precipitating a plethora of debates, articles, papers and books. Some of these even make their way into sermons, political speeches, television and radio shows, and media of specialized communication. Conceptual uncertainty makes for interesting dialog, much of it overly tedious and seemingly unending, but its exposition and analysis provide healthy catalytic stimulation for communications students and practitioners.

In this postmodern period (since World War II), the assurances of stability found in earlier periods of communication study have all but disappeared. Relativism and subjectivism affect the core of our active lives. The basic determination of the mission of our mass media is ever more difficult. The postmodern individual is found walking on sand, uncertain of the next step, testing new avenues of thought. In some ways this connects with the libertarianism of the Age of Reason, but often without the emphasis on rationality. Such an experimental and undisciplined attitude provides echoes of existentialism, with the proclivity of postmodernism to blend perspectives, to emphasize relativity, to suspect certainty, and to suggest pragmatic solutions.

At any rate I try to bring up some of the issues, myths, and ethical problems facing the mainstream media as well as bloggers and other interpersonal, specialized and private communicators of today.

The antinomies of freedom and control, individualism and communitarianism, egoism and altruism beset the communicator with their rigid hold on certainty. Successful compromise does not come easily. The tendency of today's public communicators is to hold on to as much freedom as possible and continue to ignore the communitarian urge to share this freedom with the public. A new synthesis perhaps is forming as media freedom and power clashes with public participation in communication. Another concern is the growing desire of journalists to take reportorial short cuts and to minimize public service while enthroning the lure of high salaries and profits. This can be seen in the attitudes of university students, with a few notable exceptions, who are in our journalism and communication programs.

The reader may feel that I have been overly impressed in this book by ancient Greek thinkers. Admittedly I have made much use of their thinking, but where else can one find so many catalytic ideas? The fact that Greece no longer provides such intellectual leadership to the world is probably evidence that wisdom has been progressively replaced (even in Greece) by pragmatic and materialistic concerns. Virtue is being subverted worldwide by a kind of Machiavellianism and hedonism, with a rhetorical overlay of moralism. And even a sense of fatalism, even nihilism growing out of cynicism, is casting a dark shadow over portions of the media.

Although our society is placing increasing stress on media morality, the fact is that unethical practices are not diminishing; in fact, they seem to be growing. Educational emphasis on media ethics today appears useless. Relativity and subjectivity are washing away moral certitude. Normative ethics seems too authoritarian, and one is encouraged to develop a less formalistic and less rigid moral perspective where almost any action can be approved. A spate of instinctivism and emotionalism is dimming the emphasis on rational theories of morality.

My influences and gurus for this book include many contemporary colleagues and many not so contemporary. They have impacted my thinking but bear no blame for my missteps in reason and rhetoric. In my early years as student and teacher, I was influenced by such stalwarts as Wilbur Schramm, Leslie Moeller, Raymond Nixon, Frank Luther Mott, Robert Desmond and David Manning White. In more recent years these fellow journalism educators have provided intellectual stimulation: Everette Dennis, Ralph Lowenstein, Jay Black, David Gordon, John Michael Kittross, Phil Meyer, L. John Martin, Ted Glasser, Kaarle Nordenstreng, Elizabeth Noelle-Neumann, Arnold DeBeer, Alfonso Nieto, Klaus Schoenbach, and many others.

Great thinkers of the past making a deep impression on me have been such diverse persons as Confucius, Plato and Aristotle, Augustine, Kant, Locke, Herbert Spencer, J. S. Mill, Constant, Nietzsche, Kierkegaard, Emerson, and Mencken. Even maverick thinkers such as Joseph de Maistre and Machiavelli have provided insights. Other influences have come from the writings of the early Marx, from Popper, Fromm, Korzybski, Dewey, Wittgenstein, and Habermas, as well as some of the critical theorists and communitarians.

If the reader thinks I am unrealistically pessimistic in this little book, I hope that opinion is not correct. What I am, I think, is a realistic pessimist. And this pessimism is based on recent communication history which I believe bears out my negative — at least skeptical — perspectives on the mass media. The Second Law of

Thermodynamics applied to the media system is not promising. The insidious tendency of the system to run down, to disintegrate, to lose strength (the process of entropy) tempts us to fatalism. But it can also challenge us at least to slow this process by building "islands of decreasing entropy," as Norbert Wiener called them, that will expand qualitative and moral communication, wherever we can. And who knows, the entropic process may even be stopped.

That is what I have tried to make all my courses — Entropy Stoppers 101. If journalism has an overriding mission, it seems to me that it would be to stop, or at least to slow down, the process of social entropy. I am certainly not as pessimistic as H. L. Mencken (see frontispiece), but without a doubt undisciplined, fragmented, uncooperative, destructive and immoral social action only accelerates entropy. And a public communication system that mirrors and stresses such disharmonic tendencies is unworthy of the huge financial profits it receives. In fact, it is unworthy of any respect whatsoever and the plaudits its gives itself and its functionaries are no more than putrid signs of hypocrisy.

John C. Merrill
Professor Emeritus
School of Journalism
University of Missouri–Columbia

CHAPTER 1
CONCEPTUAL UNCERTAINTY

The media of mass (or better, public) communication are not only constantly changing, they are almost indefinable. Mass media messages bombard us from every direction and demand our attention even when we fight against their power. Media range from movies to billboards, from newspapers to the Internet and television. They institutionalize messages and assail us with advertising, propaganda, news, entertainment, interpretation and analysis. They insist on being heard and on selling us products, religion, sports, celebrities, politicians, gurus and a wide assortment of atypical people.

The world of the communicator is overflowing with uncertainty. Basic terms go undefined and more complex concepts continue to spawn debate and even ideological chaos. For some, the message is the match that ignites the flames of progressive social discourse and, in many cases, of communal discord. According to others (e.g. Marshall McLuhan, 1965), the media themselves impact our lives, causing us to think and act differently than we would without them. Some say the media create our world, set our agenda, create our biases, affect our language and cement our human relationships. Others say they create tensions, foster stereotypes, exploit the gullible, divide classes, races, and religions, cause excessive spending, destroy traditional cultures and solidify big-nation hegemony.

I see the media as mechanistic extensions of human morality, in some cases socially productive and civilizing and in other cases promoting degrading and uncivil activities. I must insist, perhaps contrary to McLuhan and others, that people make the media what they are, and not the other way around. Humanity can rise above the media, but media always conform to the state of humanity. Ultimately it is the individual person who will save the world or will destroy the world. The media, however, have an ever stronger foothold of power and attempt to collectivize maverick individuals in corrals of social solidarity. Social ethics, authenticated by normative codes, is one result of this, and the allure of group cooperation and moral obedience to relativistic authority is extremely potent. This brand of media morality, predicated on majoritarian correctness, further endangers the individual person who may march to a different drumbeat.

|

Some of us hold the media responsible for many of our misfortunes and crises. We are critical of their excesses, of their free-wheeling liberty, of their exaggerations and misrepresentations, of their political biases (if we disagree with them), of their superficiality, of their vulgarity and sexploitation. In short, the American people don't seem to like the media very much.

But great numbers of them conform to the media's culture; it becomes an addiction. They expose themselves to the media, sitting for hours in movie houses, before TV screens, and reading newspapers and magazines. Right, they say, but what else do we have? We walk on broken and rough sidewalks if that's all we have. We vote for inferior candidates if we have no other choice. We expose ourselves to our media because that's all we have. If that is true, then we put media freedom (and power) above our own freedom, and that is a tragedy. Each of us always has the freedom to say "no" to the media as they are. Perhaps our freedom (and will) to evade the media would cause the media to reinvent themselves and take a higher moral road.

Whether the media are mainly instruments for social good or for social harm is an open question. But they are potent. Advertisers tell us that media are omnipresent and seemingly omniscient. They impact our thinking and our buying habits. We are all influenced in some way by them every day. At least that is true of the middle classes, people who have the education, the curiosity, and the money to get the publications and technology they need to be well-informed.

The institutionalized communicators in the United States, the public media, have a basic problem: They are hanging somewhere between being responsible for public enlightenment and democracy and being a part of a successful business. It is easy to slip into the business mode and become simply cogs in the capitalistic wheel of profit-making. Since they are somewhat protected by the Constitution, they revel in their freedom and their autonomous marketplace determination of messages. Much of this high-minded self-determinism is natural, stemming from the liberalism of the Enlightenment. And much of it is a matter of false self-importance and an acceptance of uncertain or mythological concepts.

Huge profit margins at the beginning of the 21st century have lured the media away from a basic concern for public service, and from serious content. A desire to have a large and well-qualified staff — reporters and editors — has lessened and news executives talk more and more about the bottom line. News coverage especially has suffered. Foreign news is increasingly relegated to an inferior place in the media and much of it is only a revision of what appears in other countries' newspapers. Or, it comes from a drop-by visit of a circuit-riding reporter jumping from area to area. The rationale: (a) good foreign coverage is too expensive, (b) people are not interested in it, and (c) local news should be the priority.

Entertainment in the media has mushroomed. Even the news magazines now look like *People* magazine, and most newspapers are morphing into *USA Today* look-alikes. And media directors know that entertainment sells their products. News may be important to a handful of audience members, but what sells publications and programming is entertainment. A kind of superficial patina is covering a scant core of information. Having the choice between information and entertainment, the media moguls have in the main, opted for the latter.

Institutionalized communication enterprises — that is what media are. They can, and do, participate in all kinds of message dissemination — to mass, specialized, and individualized audiences.

They dispense entertainment, information, opinion, and news — probably in that order. They dip into all social areas, albeit superficially — into business, politics, religion, sports, international relations, military concerns, medicine, crime, education, travel, the arts (drama, music, literature, painting/sculpture, architecture), and they dabble sporadically in astronomy, astrology, gardening, hobbies, weddings and deaths, environmental matters, and many other "minor" news areas. In short, the media have managed to fill almost every social interest gap one can imagine.

They are said to do wonderful things. For instance, it is widely believed that the media make possible, or at least foster, democracy. They provide, it is said, the information needed for the public to understand their society and to make intelligent decisions as to elections and the conduct of public business. This, of course, is a worthy objective. But it is really little more than a myth, constructed mainly by the media themselves — especially by the so-called news media.

Little evidence has reached me that the media are seriously interested in democracy. As institutions they themselves do not exemplify democracy, having as they do a very hierarchical (Platonic) structure that is basically authoritarian. They provide little information or suggestions as to how their audiences can increase their ability to affect government. Major players in politics — namely the two parties — crowd out other political entities in the media's coverage. Those media with ideological identities are little more than platforms for a narrow-focused propaganda, either praising the Democrats or the Republicans, the liberals or the conservatives. And those with no ideological identities thrash around in all directions, their messages having no unity or coherence, trying to be everything to everyone. They end up being nothing to anyone.

Or something less than helpful to everyone.

The people do not rule, really. What we have is a "lobbyocracy" rather than a democracy. Or at least we have a system where our elected plutocrats too often are bought off by the lobbyists of the big corporations and institutions. And our media basically ignore this, giving little or no attention to the intricacies and anti-democratic tendencies in the halls of government.

Opinion is cheap and easy to come by. News is expensive and hard to come by. Opinion mainly reinforces a public's opinion or tries to change it. News provides information upon which sound opinion can be formed. Media are tending toward the easy alternative — opinion — much less difficult and expensive to get. Mix this opinion with a heady brew of entertainment and you have the bottom-line formula for postmodern journalism.

Even though business concerns tend increasingly to dominate the news media, the basic philosophy of individual journalists can — and should — have an important part to play in shaping the media's policies. Much at this point could be said about the education of journalists. Certainly it has changed greatly since I began teaching in 1951 when most students were idealists and language-lovers and looked on journalism largely as a public service. Many were strong students of English in high school and wanted an outlet for their devotion to writing. They also were students who wanted to have an impact on their society in a positive way.

By the 1980s this was changing, and by 2006 it had changed, for the most part. Young aspiring media people, instead of being language-lovers, have become "technologists." Instead of jousting with windmills, they are largely satisfied to blow about on the winds of nihilism. Instead of public servants, they have become corporate functionaries or private entrepreneurs. Instead of objectivists, they have become subjectivists and relativists, and instead of journalists they have become communicators.

Students today are going into television and into public relations and advertising where they can make more money. Inheriting the baby-boomer lifestyle, most of them are not satisfied with the modest salaries offered by newspapers. And on television, they are mainly interested in how they look, their voice quality, and their ability to talk while smiling. The "news readers" are more important than the "news gatherers." One astute media critic, Joseph Epstein (2006), has pointed out that Americans regard journalists as unaccountable kibitzers who spread dissension, increase pressure on their audiences, and make trouble. In our "dumbed down" world, he says, there is little evidence that our newspapers provide an oasis of taste.

It is small wonder that an emphasis on information is decreasing in our media and assorted entertainment is mushrooming. It is small wonder that op-ed pieces and lively letters-to-the-editor are commanding more attention in the print media today. And it is small wonder that what we once called "hard news" is disappearing into a miasma of popular, brain-numbing features. Journalism students are learning that sensation and infotainment is journalism's future, and, by and large, this is where the money is.

Various studies that my students and I have conducted through the years have shown clearly that the media contain very little substantial news about the democratic process, about alternatives to the status quo, about the background and character of candidates, about complex political and social issues, about ways citizens can have a regular impact on government, about the workings of various government agencies and organizations, or about the moral ineptitudes of "public servants." In short, the media mainly deal with superficialities of government, shining their light on the personalities of various politicians and their off-beat entertainment-oriented activities. As the elderly woman in the popular TV commercial said: "Where's the beef?"

As pointed out earlier, "the beef" should be instrumental in expanding democracy. Being democratic is better than talking democracy. But are these media institutions really interested in reaching all segments of society? Do they really want social equality and maximum public enlightenment? I doubt it very much. They don't even support democracy in their own internal affairs, spreading the editorial gospel to the conforming underclass of functionaries. Like Plato's philosophers, they don't trust democratically selected functionaries and claim they love meritocracy — as long as they manage to be a part of it.

However, in spite of Platonic objections, the concept of deliberative democracy is seen today as a good thing and American journalists generally embrace it — at least in theory. Democracy is said to enable the people to have significant input in government and to determine policy through deliberation on the issues. Media observers such as Bill Moyers and Robert McChesney maintain that democracy cannot exist without an informed public. This may be true theoretically, but it does not work that way. The media fail to give people the information and interpretation with which to deliberate. And the people have little chance to make their weak and spotty deliberation heard in high places. The fact is that only a small group of intellectuals and practical politicians have any real impact on public issues. If observers like Moyers are right, then we must concede that little if any democracy exists in the United States.

II

Among the criticisms hurled at the media is that they are biased. The media largely refuse to admit any bias at all. It is this, more than the bias, that infuriates the astute audience member.

Media are full of biases. Media managers and staffers throughout the hierarchy have their values. This is natural, and it is strange that media people would deny their biases. I even met an editor recently who was biased against bias. The American press, from the very beginning, has projected its various biases on the people. It has been, in many respects, "postmodern," even before the term became popular. Behind American journalism is the philosophical notion that no one perspective or view of reality has ultimate dominance. At the end of the so-called postmodern (pre-futuristic?) age, one wonders if a monism of basic meaning will return to the world of communication. But perhaps such a situation has never existed, with the world always being multi-perspectival.

Biases have solidified around various communicative persons and factions. There were the views of Socrates and Plato, of Confucius and Lao Tzu, of Augustine and Aquinas. And then there were the Hegelians and those who followed Kierkegaard. There were the Marxists and there were the Adam Smiths. And more recently we have Fox television and we have CNN. Differing interpretations have proliferated and often contradictory "frames" have stressed different aspects of a story. But press people themselves hate to admit this, and maintain that they are basically objective and neutral.

Jacques Derrida, a French philosopher who has been a leader in inter-subjective postmodernism, has argued that interpretation is part of reality. True there has been some stress given to interpretative reporting. But this has been a difficult idea for American journalism, steeped as reporters are in keeping themselves out of the report. And it would probably take a Freud or a Jung to properly interpret interpretative reporting. Increasingly, however, journalists are beginning to recognize the impossibility (and the weaknesses) of so-called objectivity. Now it is generally believed that when a person buys a newspaper, he or she buys a point of view. Or perhaps better, when a person listens to, or reads, a reporter's story, what is received is a point of view.

Postmodern thinking has brought home the idea of a multiplicity of possible meanings and has heightened a suspicious attitude. Readers should be suspicious of news reports. Reporters should be suspicious of news sources, of other reporters, and of themselves and their perspectives. The postmodern position is this: have a suspicion of any single meaning for an event, and recognize the multiplicity of interpretations. No story is objective. In short, the individual interpretation is part of, not separate from, the story. Postmodernism does not depreciate the power of the media; in fact, the emergence of this new social order is largely determined —or at least sped up — by the media and popular culture. Contemporary society reveals that most established certainties and traditions of earlier periods are disappearing. As ethicist Larry Leslie (2004, p. 11) has astutely noted, public communicators have "gone beyond the modern age to the postmodern era" where they are encountering moral and social problems they are ill-equipped to handle.

So the intriguing question arises: Just what can the reporter or the audience member know for certain? What is the true story? It seems that the old Miltonic belief that the truth will win out in a contest with falsehood has vanished. How can one know the truth? How can the news consumer separate the truth from the interpretation? The answer to all these questions is: It can't really be done. One must accept certain event-interpretations on faith. The truth may, or may not, manifest itself from the pluralism of viewpoints.

Managers of the media thrive on the accoutrements of prestige and power. Tucked away in their stately offices with their carpeted space and fancy desks, they are — even to their own workers — more like kings than democrats. Even the recent short-lived emphasis on public (a.k.a. civic) journalism, a manifestation of democratic interest, did not impress the media moguls. Not wanting to share power with the people, the media leaders have warned about unqualified public determination in programming and editorial decision-making. There is considerable Platonic aristocracy to be found in the top levels of every communication medium. Bad idea, they say, to get the people involved in journalism. This would simply popularize and undermine the quality of public communication. After a brief but insignificant ripple on the media scene, public journalism has all but faded away in the face of continuing capitalistic elitism and press plutocracy.

Media have largely determined "social and political realities" and have increased knowledge in every area, but they failed, as communication scholar Hanno Hardt has written, to improve the intellectual level of the public to a point that society can deal with the world's complexity. American media rankle at being called "propagandistic," although there is little doubt that they are. From ideological perspectives of the news and outright opinion, to overt advertising messages, the media spew out a steady stream of biased, persuasive material. Hardt makes the pointed observation that mass communication, from the invention of the printing press on, has led away from authentic individual expression to the institutional inauthenticity of the twentieth century. Quoting Max Horkheimer, Hardt notes (2004) that the media "fetter the individual" to prescribed modes of thinking and buying habits. In short, they have institutionalized propaganda and substituted public robotization for personal decision-making.

Public messages are largely propagandistic — persuasive, action-oriented, and deceptive. They generally serve some special interest, some ideology, some religion, some institution, some political position, or some special group. There may be some neutral, simply informational messages, but they are few. Most messages are tailored, often in very subtle ways, to capture our minds and our allegiances.

They, directly or indirectly, invite us to take an action — buy a product, vote for a certain person or party, accept a position, join an organization, participate in a demonstration, attend a certain university.

In America, unlike in many authoritarian countries, we have a diversity of propaganda. Often, therefore, one propaganda will cancel out another. What the audience members do is to seek out congenial propaganda, that which reinforces their beliefs and inclinations. Propaganda, it must be admitted, is hard to define and harder to detect. Perhaps the best we can say about propaganda is that is persuasive, intentional, selfish, deceptive and action-oriented. It is rather typical of many concepts related to mass communication that they stimulate public dialog but are semantically problematic.

CHAPTER 2

VIEWS ON THE NEWS

Basic public communication concepts such as news, objectivity, truth, journalism, reporter, magazine, newspaper, bias, propaganda, mass, public opinion, profession, media, and media ethics — these and many others await meaningful definitions.

One of the most troublesome of the concepts is "news." What some would call news could be thought of as entertainment to others. For example, is the sports section of a newspaper news or entertainment? Or, beyond that, cannot a hard news story (like the August-September 2005 hurricanes in the Gulf of Mexico) be entertaining, even a kind of *Schadenfreude*, for many people? Some advertisers claim that advertising is news. Telling the public of a new product is information not known previously, so they say, "It's news." That's stretching it in the best (or worst) tradition of advertising. If we're not careful every message will be advertising. At any rate, everyone knows that when a person is identified as an advertiser, this is not the same as saying that he or she is a journalist.

The very concept of news is problematic. I remember well the textbooks that insisted that an event had to be reported in order to be news. News was not out there waiting to be reported. The hotel fire may be something — an event — but it was not news until it appeared as a report in a news medium. It makes one wonder if a newspaper is a newspaper before it is circulated and read by someone. Such definitional problems are at least interesting.

Many will say they are not really important — that all this definition business is only "a matter of semantics." Of course this is correct. Definitions are matters of meaning. But a concern for semantics is important in a practical world, and if we do not pay attention to what people and things are called, we strain the limits of cognition and fall into an abyss of misunderstanding. A rose may smell just as sweet if called a table, but it could cause serious dinner problems. A newspaper may resemble a magazine, but it is different — and the careful communicator will use the proper name when referring to it. Oh, well — some antics with semantics!

I

Journalists generally claim they know news when they see it. Textbooks are replete with lists of characteristics of news — proximity, timeliness, prominence and such. It is true that there is a rough common concept of news throughout the media world. But there are also significant differences. The opening of a new hotel: news or not? Depending on a number of factors, it may or may not be. A storm that wastes a city and dislodges thousands of refugees: news or not? No doubt about it — news, big news. A football game planned months ahead. News? For some it is, for others — entertainment. Or a preview to being entertained. A deer hit by a car in the middle of a city? A child falling into a well? Several observers who say they have seen a UFO? A mayor's wife who crashes into a street sign and bends a fender? A homeless person who collapses on the sidewalk? A weather prediction? Just what is news?

"It all depends," the journalist would say. Surely that is correct — it depends on so many related factors that it is impossible to answer such questions. We do know that, in the real world of the media, news is whatever journalists want to publish as news. At least it is news for their purposes, regardless of what the audience members may think of it. News is not necessarily timely; it does not have to relate to prominent people; it does not have to be significant; it does not have to be sensational or negative; it does not have to contain information that is truthful.

News historically has been considered, in spite of semantic difficulty, the core substance of journalism. But from a realistic perspective, news today has lost its primary status. It has evolved into infotainment, into personality profiles, and into soft and slushy stories, somewhere between news features and entertainment, between polemic and propaganda. The citizen looking for credible information about government policy, about political candidates, about the intricacies of national economics, about what he or she can do to access the system, and about serious topics needed by democratic people to have their voices heard — this citizen will get little help from the hodge-podge and contradictory media with their emphasis on advertisement and entertainment.

We still use the terms "newscasts" (for TV and radio) and talk about "newspapers," but these are misnomers. News programs on the broadcast media are really happy talk revolving around personal opinion and entertainment features, and only about 10 percent of newspaper space is given over to what has traditionally been called news. The other 90 percent is consumed by advertising, features, editorials, columns, letters, puzzles, and an assortment of entertainment-oriented items and pictures.

So poorly are the masses of the American people informed that it seems time for the unrealistic belief that the media are essential for democracy to be put to rest. This belief may well disappear as we enter the rapidly advancing Age of the Internet and the possibility of direct balloting into that Great Computer in the Nation's Capital. However, it is well to realize that instant voting possibilities and computer-driven bombardment of messages do not assure credibility or democratic reality. The new world of communication may only serve to spread instantaneous ignorance and confusion.

Still said by many to be an ideal is the concept of full-context, thorough news-presentation. This is a very problematic concept, most often propounded within the news media. It is that stories (or reporters) can be objective. Such a belief rests on theory, not practice. It is no more than an ideal, valuable indeed for reporters. Schools of journalism often talk about "objective reporting" and an "objective reporter." Of course, a major problem is semantic; different people have varied definitions for an abstract term like "objectivity," as the general semanticist Alfred Korzybski (1933) stressed in his writings.

II

Objectivity is one of the most misunderstood terms in journalism. Many (like most postmodernists of today) call it naïve empiricism; others refer to it as an unachievable ideal; others maintain that it should not be used at all. And others, more traditional, say simply that an objective story (or a reporter) is one that "tries to be" reliable, not perfect but generally credible. In spite of its vagueness, the term has a positive connotation.

The concept of objectivity comes from a scientific orientation, not a more artistic one, as C. P. Snow has noted. But the idea that a reporter has to be neutral or detached from the event being reported has lost much of its meaning. Postmodernism, with its emphasis on analysis and interpretation woven into a factual framework, has played a large part.

Postmodernism negates absolutism and certainty and proposes little more than experimental progressivism. E. O. Wilson has written (1998, p. 38) that the main difference between postmodern thinking and that of the Age of Reason is this: "Enlightenment thinkers believed we can know everything, and radical postmodernists believe we can know nothing." Naturally, then, the postmodernist would question the very concept of objective journalism.

Objectivity was the American journalist's creed in the second half of the 20th century but no longer. A kind of subjectivized objectivity has made considerable inroads. As Erich Fromm discusses it in *Man for Himself*, objectivity requires more than seeing an event dispassionately and neutrally. The observer needs to become related in some way to that which is being reported. The nature of the object and that of the observer must be merged, and they are equally important — that is, if we want to get at what constitutes objectivity. It is not, he says, scientific objectivity, synonymous with being detached with no interest or care.

During the second half of the 20th century, emotional, involved, sentimental reporting took a prominent place on the media scene, especially in television. Teary-eyed Walter Cronkite choking up as he reported the first man stepping on the moon. Overwhelmed reporters trying to deal with the terrorist attack on the Twin Towers in Manhattan on 9/11/01. And the weeping, emotional interview (with Louisiana Sen. Mary Landrieu) conducted by CNN reporter Anderson Cooper in the aftermath of Hurricane Katrina in August 2005. The revolt against journalistic objectivity appears to get ever stronger.

Even with the statements of those who, like Fromm, advise bringing the observer into the concept of objectivity, and like broadcaster Anderson Cooper who does intrude in the event, the idea of subjective objectivity is still problematic. Reportorial intrusion is, of course, natural to some degree. The observer, of course, is subjective and his or her report will reflect this subjectivity — the process of straining reality through the filters of the observer's perceptions. This colors the report. Add to that the inadequacies of language itself to reflect reality accurately (Korzybski, 1933). A report may be truthful but not objective. It is always incomplete, although its facts may be accurate. Even the story of a speech that includes every word the speaker says is nonobjective in its incompleteness. Gestures, facial expressions, thoughts not spoken, tongue-in-cheek statements, and the like are all part of "the story of the speech" and go unreported. In addition, the audience's reaction is really unknown and unreported, although part of the speech story.

Many journalists (and audience members) simply don't care about all this reality talk. Audiences generally want to "believe" news reports but don't expect them to reproduce completely the event described. They are satisfied with the bits and pieces of reality and do not expect to get the whole story. We observe, we rely on memory, and we seek testimony from others. That's how we know what we know. Not much but perhaps enough. Is objectivism a myth? Maybe so, but most people don't care. It could be that all journalism is a myth and should be called public mythology instead of journalism. At least we can say that journalism provides little more than the shadows on Plato's cave wall. Rationalist or empiricist, the journalists (and we) stumble through the darkness seeing little of reality. Probably a good thing because the stark brightness of reality would quite likely be too much for us.

Unlike Bishop Berkeley, the great idealist of Britain, I think reality is "out there," and it is there whether or not we see it or sense it. The journalist may never get it completely in the story, but it's out there. It happens; it is — this regardless of being reported. The Transcendental level of truth, the complete truth, the truth in all its fullness. This Truth with a capital letter, is always beyond the journalist. It cannot be reached. But portions of it break through into the empirical world and even the poorest journalist can find some of this potential truth. That is evidently what journalists mean when they speak of objective reporting. The pure facts, however scarce they are — that is objectivity for many journalists. We know that the reporter's subjectivity enters the picture — often bending or interpreting the pure facts, thereby adding a subjective dimension to the objective report. But that's all right; that's natural. Getting a really objective story is impossible. For one thing, the subjectivity of the persons involved in the story (the reporter and the one being reported on) is part of the "objective" reality of the story — and no reporter, even with the help of a psychiatrist, can ever come close to doing justice to that.

If a report is to be credible to the audience, it should be verifiable. At least that is the more scientific belief about it. That would mean, of course, that the reporter should provide the audience member with information as to how this information can be checked out. As a reader, for example, to whom can I go to check on the validity of the story? Some source must be able to attest to the story's accuracy. That means that, if legitimate news, the story must provide a means to substantiate its contents. This would mean, say many journalism critics, that a source must be given. Many newspapers are, for example, now requiring that their reporters give the names of sources. *The New York Times*, for example, in 2005 introduced a new policy stating that use of anonymous sources would henceforth be the exception rather than the rule. It seems there will be fewer "deep throats" of the Woodward and Bernstein era.

But there is the opposite view: that news is news and a report is a report without a source being given. If I write that the Picard

Building burned to the ground last night and I do not give a source for that fact, this omission does not detract from the story's truth. The building burned and it is news regardless of whether I say that the fire chief said it burned. The case of a news story based on a statement from some government official is more problematic. For example: "Property taxes will be doubled next year, a city official said today." This is not like a burned building out there for everyone to see; it is a report of what somebody said. How do we as audience members check it out? We can't, really, so we recognize that the source of the statement is very important to the story itself.

Also, as the argument goes, if a reporter promises a source not to reveal his or her name, then it is incumbent on the reporter not to do so. In addition to the ethical problem with breaking the promise, there is the practical problem of possibly losing that source for future stories. In any case, the revelation of sources is a real problem in journalism. Who said something is, indeed, important — sometimes very important. But, on the other hand, what was said was indeed said, regardless of who said it. But, in my opinion, the importance of naming sources outweighs the importance of hiding sources. For in the last analysis the source's name is an integral part of the story and, therefore, ideally should be included.

III

News in a theoretical sense is quite different from news in a real sense. More than one hundred codes of ethics from around the world were examined in 1985 (Cooper et al., 1985) and the expectations of what news should be were found to be similar if not identical. In reality news is almost anything. (Within a journalistic frame, news is what is presented by a news outlet, not what is told to a neighbor over the back fence.) It is, in fact, anything that an editor wants to publish as news. I conceive of news in a broader sense — what I don't already know and hear from any source is news. My neighbor's back fence information may well be as newsworthy as any put out by a public medium. If I am right, then we are all news reporters. But that does not mean we are all journalists.

What is the basic nature of journalistic news? In theory, at least in traditional idealistic press theory, news reports should be (1) information needed by an audience, (2) reporting that avoids harm to the society, and (3) factual, accurate, balanced, relevant, and complete. Reinforcing these three objectives of news was Deni Elliott's argument (1988) that these three objectives are found everywhere and universally have been non-negotiable.

Well, I'm not sure about that. In my experience these "requirements" for news have definitely been negotiable in many cultures and political systems. Even in the United States such norms are questionable. Let's look at the first one: that news must satisfy a need. Perhaps nine-tenths of the news today is not "needed" by its audience, unless one defines "need" in a very broad and perhaps psychological sense. The second objective — providing information that does no social harm. Ideal, perhaps, but not even mildly realistic. News abounds that does some kind of social harm, and one wonders if the journalist should even try to predict the consequences of stories. Unconcern with consequences (the Kantian stance) is the natural and, for me, preferable position for the reporter. And, the third: that the stories be factual, accurate, balanced, relevant, and complete. Impossible! No news reporting can fulfill these requirements. Maybe some in some instances, but never all of them.

This does not mean, however, that the news writer should not try. Different degrees of actuality and objectivity exist, and the best reporters are those who come closest to the ideal. Objectivity may be a myth, but it is a useful one that gives the reporter a goal to strive for. Semanticist Korzybski (1933) used to say, "The map is not the territory," but there are better and worse maps and mapmakers. News reporters need to go beyond the mountains and rivers, beyond the continents and oceans of their stories; the good ones will fill in with less dominant, but important, hills and streams, countries and seas and lakes. At the same time reporters can restrict what Joseph Epstein (2006) has called a "mighty cataract of inessential information that threatens to drown us all."

News is not objectivity. News is a selection from objectivity. It is a story that is strained through the perceptions of the reporter, mingling biases and judgments of the reporter with the cold facts of the event. Many reporters think they are objective if they are neutral, dispassionate, balanced and accurate. Professor Ted Glasser (1992, 181) makes a good point when he says that often journalists claim neutrality in order to defend against criticism that they are biased, but in the process they deny "their passion and their perspective." And "balance" will not suffice. Always there are more than two sides to a question; giving two opponents equal time or space does not assure balance or fairness.

Often one side stands far above the other in truth and insight. The good news reporter will recognize this and get it into the story. A biased story? No. An unbalanced story? Yes.

IV

Another problem with news is the poor use of language by those who are reporting it.

Our schools and departments of journalism are not stressing brevity, conciseness, simplicity and organization. Nor are they trying to instill a love for the language. English departments have virtually given up on trying to teach composition. Speech departments are not refining the pronunciation, enunciation and the importance of good speech habits. For those going into print or broadcast journalism, it is mainly left to the journalism programs — the undergraduate programs — to try to remedy the generally awful language usage. I must say that many are concerned. But, by and large, the language deficiencies of students have all but overburdened even the most dedicated teachers. But, at least with undergraduates, there is hope.

Graduate education, however, is quite different. These programs in journalism and communication actually encourage bad writing. I would warn the conscientious writer to avoid graduate courses if at all possible. If they must take such courses, they must try to ignore as much as possible the gobblygook and affected language that the "research-oriented" professors so much admire. Theory and research have joined hands with sociological jargon to push upon students a kind of mystical and secret world of academic "spin" that makes the shallow seem deep and the simple seem complex. To be fair, it must be said that here and there are graduate professors (mainly historians) doing a good job with their students. Some very good histories and biographies are being written, but they are on the decrease in our graduate studies programs.

Prospective news writers, if they want a graduate degree, fall prey to the dominant theoreticians and statisticians whose objective is to get grants, present their papers at conferences, and share their esoterica with other academics. What is important, obviously, is to get published, and maybe even have your article cited in someone else's article. The writer learns to hide (obfuscate?) meaning and resort to impressive, pseudo-language that gives the thesis, article, or book a sense of deep thought and seriousness. This practice can ruin, and probably has ruined, the writing ability of many reporters.

Reporting research should be done as well as reporting news events. There is no reason, other than researcher self-inflation and affectation, for the report of a research project to be difficult to read and understand. It is strange how many researchers seem to equate jargon with thoughtful rhetoric and obscure and tautological construction with careful reporting. One reason for such obscurity in research reporting is that either the research is unimportant or no definite conclusion has been reached. Fancy language and inflated construction can often hide the absence of substance.

Poor writing is one thing. Journalistic bias is another. As to the political orientation of today's students in journalism education programs, I will say only what the surveys tell us: that nearly 80 percent of those surveyed classified themselves as "liberal." A similar percentage of practicing journalists (at least in the big newspapers and TV stations) say they are liberal and Democrat in politics. This, perhaps, is not surprising because journalism draws socially conscious, public-service types who desire to "make a difference."

In my more than a half century in journalism education, I have observed the predominantly liberal bias of my fellow professors. And it is not surprising that if students hear this perspective day after day, month after month, it is going to affect their ideology. If one doubts what I am saying, just take a look at the textbooks used in journalism courses, the names of sources in the indexes, and listen to media people who give speeches in universities and are keynoters at academic journalism conferences.

I am well aware that talk radio is dominated by a swarm of Rush Limbaughs, pushing the agenda of conservatives and Republicans. I know also that the grassroots press is largely conservative. But the colleges and universities are filled with liberal professors, hiring their own kind, denigrating the traditional values of society, and pushing students constantly into postmodern relativity and critical theory where everything (except liberal values) is constantly questioned. During my more than fifty years in academe, even my interest in such thinkers like Friedrich Nietzsche, Leo Strauss, Eric Voegelin, Friedrich Hayek, and Frank Meyer has made me, among my faculty colleagues, a kind of dinosaur wandering in the wastelands of Germanic conservatism. What I am really is a Goldwater-Marxist sponge, trying to soak up wisdom from all quarters.

I have had a firm belief that I should provide students with viewpoints of articulate and thoughtful people from all across the political spectrum. I must admit that it is much harder to find conservative journalists and professors to quote than liberal ones, but I have been moderately successful. The opinion itself, not the source, is what is important to me, but I have found that who says something is a very powerful factor in the belief system of students. So, it has been (not often) that I will, when speaking to a basically conservative audience (and there are some), attribute an obviously liberal quote from Ted Kennedy to conservative Bill Buckley, and note the positive response of the audience. At any rate, in my opinion, teachers, students, and journalists should all consider substance and ideas rather than being influenced by an affinity to a person making a statement. And journalists should seek out people with rational concepts and ideas and not the same old worn-out spokesman for certain groups — like Jesse Jackson or Pat Buchanan, or Gloria Steinem or Jerry Falwell.

More voices need to be heard in the public forum. In the universities, it is important for students and introvert-professors (if there are any) to speak up, to present their views, to have their voices heard. And more people in their communities need to enter the public conversation. It is not easy when one feels in the minority, when one thinks that his or her ideas are not the dominant ones. One is prone to keep quiet. The German scholar and pollster, Elisabeth Noelle-Neumann, has referred to this as the "spiral of silence" — the tendency of people in a group to keep silent when the force of opinion is going against them. How refreshing it is to hear dissenting opinions, opposing viewpoints, differing concepts. I have noted in some of my classes that a Chinese student, for instance, is reluctant to enter the conversation or to ask a question when she senses that what she might say would not be popular. Outside class, however, she may share her ideas with me, and I am always sorry that the class did not have the opportunity to hear her.

CHAPTER 3

MEDIA MELANGE

One of the main reasons for the conceptual uncertainty (as with the term "news") we have just looked at is that the relationship of media to authority varies so greatly throughout the world. If the intricacies of language don't perplex us, then the complexity of differing media systems will. Several theoretical media-support possibilities stem from political ideologies that add to mission and moral differences. Then, within each theoretical and actual system of media support, there are at least three substantial "types" of media. All of these theoretical and intricate media configurations, with their varied and ever-changing features, tend to confuse, frustrate and even anger mass communicators everywhere.

Many scholars say there are four theories of the press, getting their typology largely from the Hutchins Commission and a mid-20th-century book by Siebert, Peterson, and Schramm. Although the concept has been severely criticized (i.e. by Christians, Ferre, et al.) for being ethno-centric (Western) and for not being semantically clear, this "four theories" concept has remained firmly in the literature and is taught widely in the classroom. Here we have the authoritarian, the libertarian, the communist, and the social responsibility "theories." I have maintained that the last one does not belong with the other three — that the authoritarian, the libertarian and the communist are all identifiable in actual societies, whereas the fourth is not connected to any one society. Also I have maintained that the first three theories are all responsible to their particular societies (Merrill, 1974). In addition, the question comes up: Who is to define social responsibility? All in all it is a strange typology of three descriptive press systems and one extremely vague system.

My critique of the four theories was in turn criticized by others. A common accusation was that I called the communist (leftist) and the authoritarian (rightist) theories both "socially responsible." Certainly I was doing that, but I was not endorsing either of them or saying that they were moral theories. I was simply saying that, within the context of their politico-economic systems, they were "responsible." The communist media system, for instance, would have been irresponsible to its society had it permitted wealthy capitalists to own media and further widen the class differences or to permit a free press to endanger the stability of the party-oriented society.

I

So, I think that in this sense media systems can be looked at as all socially responsible to their systems. But since those days when I made such a suggestion, I have come to believe that there is but one really meaningful press theory (or system): the authoritarian system.

It seems to me that this is a more realistic way to look at media systems, none of which is really free of some kind of control or direction. It also avoids the labeling stigma of some systems being more authoritarian than others They are all authoritarian — just in different ways.

In order to study any press system, one needs to find the locus of the authority. And there is always some authority — or authorities (for often several combine in giving direction to the media). In the United States, I would suggest that the media authority is a combination of media owners and advertisers. Here we are talking about a capitalist system with a heavy overlap of Enlightenment libertarianism.

In fact, this press autonomy system is the one of the four theories (Siebert, et al.) called the libertarian theory. It is a market theory, a *laissez faire* concept, where media plutocrats rule over the press. The authority is not the government, but the media people themselves. Of course, they are influenced greatly by the advertisers and by public opinion, so that in spite of their separation from government control, the public media have an authority. And at least in theory, they provide the greatest message diversity of all press systems.

The State-Party is another authoritarian media system. The authority here comprises the leaders of the state and/or party. An autocrat (like a monarch) may control the media through control of the state apparatus or a party (such as in Vietnam or Cuba). This is definitely state control and there is little or no chance that much diversity or freedom will exist in such a system. Advantages would be that policies cannot be delayed or disputed by the media, that central planning can proceed smoothly and expeditiously, and that public opinion can be molded to fit the needs of the governmental leadership. Relativists are not particularly bothered by such a state controlled system. Their view is represented by cultural anthropologist Ruth Benedict, who contends that cultural differences determine ethics. So what is an improper system for the United States is not an improper system for Cuba.

Even a theoretically democratic country like Japan can hide under this second type, having a closer connection or partnership with government than is clearly visible from the outside. Press clubs are common in Japan, and through them government has enormous influence over the newspapers. The press club system institutionalizes and enforces cooperative relations between journalists and the establishment, encourages self-censorship, gives journalists a sense of elitism, discourages independent investigative reporting, and encourages boring and unhelpful news. Writing in 2004 *(A Public Betrayed)*, Adam Gamble and Takesato Watanabe cite these elite journalists' organizations as the main cause of Japan's "corrupt news media." They lead to interlocking sub-rosa relationships that destroy real press freedom and pollute the entire news stream.

The two systems discussed above (media owners and state-party) can be empirically studied; they have existed and do exist today. A look at the United States and several European countries will provide examples of the first. And throughout the world — in a large number of nations — can be found the second type of authoritarianism — in

China, in North Korea, in Cuba, in Saudi Arabia, in Egypt, in Syria, and in most of the African countries.

II

Let me suggest several other possible or theoretical systems that, so far as I can tell, have never been tried. But I recognize that they could work for media-support or authoritarian control. What might these authorities be?

First I would consider a populist/democratic media control system. The authority here would rest with the people through their elected news directors, editors and publishers.

Idealistic as this may seem, it would be possible and would make the press far more democratic than is the plutocratic press of modern America. Just how this would be done is understandably a big question. And an immediate objection to it would be that the people know little about journalism and could not elect the best people for the job.

This criticism has much validity, but no more really than trying to justify a system whereby we elect politicians to public office (e.g. the success of the extremist Hamas party in Palestine in elections in 2006). Would not a democratic media system put elected people in leadership positions? Journalists or media persons would campaign for media posts and people would choose their favorites. Such a system might be compared to the possibility of a university faculty choosing their deans and president, or to students choosing their faculty. Such a populist/democratic concept of media authority could, of course, only be possible in a country with substantial faith in the wisdom of the people.

Another possible system of state leadership and the media is a theocratic/religious authoritarianism. Here we have as the guiding authority of the society a holy book and/or religious leaders. Such a system is possible, at least for a short term, as we saw in Afghanistan with the Taliban Muslim leadership in the late 1990s. And it can be argued that there are many Muslim countries, especially in the Middle East, that are ruled by a combination of religious leaders (e.g., mullahs, ayatollahs, muftis) and the particular state ruler (e.g., president, king) at the time. Going back in European history, one might also say that a similar authoritarianism existed with the Holy Roman Empire. And today we can see it in the Vatican State where *L'Osservatore Romano* and other Roman Catholic information media are controlled by theocratic authority. In the Arabic world, as in the Holy Roman world, this type of authoritarianism can provide considerable stability and order to the society. However, as in any other of the authoritarian systems, cliques and sects develop and theocrats disagree, but in general this system would ensure social stability and viable governance.

Another type of authoritarianism related to the media could possibly exist: a subsidized media system. An entire media system could be financed by wealthy citizens, institutions and foundations. This would be different from the first (owner-advertiser) system discussed for, in this one, there would be no need for advertising. And the authority would be the subsidizer(s). Of course, this concept could overlap with the state-party system in that the subsidizer might be the party. The subsidizer could also be the national treasury itself, with the funding coming from tax money. But this system and its possible splintered possibilities would not appeal to the libertarian who would see the monopolization of communication by the subsidizer. But, like the others, this system would be authoritarian with, in this case, the subsidizer having the power and the authority.

III

Now, we come to the last of my authoritarian systems: the intellectual-elitist. Here we draw heavily on Plato and his *Republic*, mentioned elsewhere on these pages.

The wise, well-trained, virtuous, intelligent, socially oriented leaders (Plato: philosopher kings) could be called "Journalistic Philosophers." They would be the authorities. All levels of media workers would have their distinct duties and would perform them in a highly efficient and disciplined manner.

The Philosopher-Editor, for example, would be a generalist,

having a broad, but deep, liberal education. He or she would also have a firm knowledge of communication practice and theory and an overarching understanding of technology. This authority would provide practical and moral guidance for the media system or any one of its units.

Like Plato's philosopher king, the journalist-philosopher would be paid a modest salary. An elitist, yes, but not an isolated, unconcerned one. And certainly not one obsessed with making huge profits and buying up other properties.

But then, just how would such a system be financed? Here is the biggest weakness, of course. Without a doubt it would have to be combined with the subsidized system, with someone or group of wise financiers who would be willing to provide at least part of the funds and give editorial freedom to the meritocratic philosopher-editors.

Just how such a Philosopher-Journalist would be placed in an authoritarian position would have to be worked out. But it surely would not be the result of a democratic process. It would be a strictly meritocratic operation, seeking inherent intelligence, wisdom, education, leadership ability and moral superiority. This Platonic system would basically be an "aristocracy" (direction by the best), the system that Thomas Jefferson advocated — one that provided for the selection of the *aristoi* into positions of leadership. Jefferson believed, perhaps somewhat naively, that a democracy could select such superior persons. Just how the aristocratic leader in Plato's philosopher system or Nietzsche's *Uebermensch* (Overman) system would get selected for leadership is not clear. But it is obvious that they would not chosen by democratic vote. .

Such a Platonic-Nietzschean system certainly would assume special knowledge by some. Editors should be editors. Reporters should be reporters. These special people, whether they attended journalism school or not, would have journalistic understanding that the ordinary citizen would not have. It would be dangerous, possibly destructive, to journalism if "the people" were to demand a voice in running the media. The Greek historian Thucydides (Thorson, 1963, p. 27), tells us how, through a kind of class warfare, an emerging democracy ruined ancient Greece. Politicians, left and right, boasted that they were devoted to the community, and they took refuge in high-sounding phrases to achieve odious ends. The masses, feeling insecure, demanded a greater voice in policy, and, as a result, inefficient government developed which ended Greek political and cultural domination.

Today the postmodern emphasis on democratization of journalism has similarities to the weakening of the Athenian state. If meritocracy (where it obtains) in the press hierarchy is overshadowed by citizen-intrusion into content determination, it makes one wonder if journalism will not fade away. Communitarians of the public journalism type, in their rush to diminish the power of capitalistic media managers, may well universalize the concept of "journalism" and destroy knowledgeable leadership.

Since there is such a mélange of media relationships with power throughout the world, it is small wonder that little global agreement exists as to functions or mission (dealt with later in this essay). A theocratic press will have different functions from a party press, and a libertarian or autonomous press will see its range of activities in a far different way than would a subsidized press.

Having said this, I believe that most of the press-power systems discussed briefly above would likely have three audience types (intellectual, practical, illiterate) in mind and would have segments or units that would represent three types of media discussed in the next section: class, mass, crass. Exceptions might be the theocratic media system and the journalistic philosopher system. They would, rather consistently, tailor their messages to the religious community and the intellectual community, respectively.

The media owners/advertising system would naturally want to appeal to the widest audience possible. The state-party system would aim at the power structure but would also want to provide something for all sectors of society. The subsidized system, although it could be very narrow in its offerings, would probably want to provide something for all segments of society.

CHAPTER 4
CLASS, MASS AND CRASS MEDIA

Let us turn now to what I call the media-audience pyramid, describing the types of media (and their audiences) at the top of the pyramid, down through the mid-section of the pyramid, and on down to the lowest (and broadest) section of the pyramid.

In most media systems, as we have seen, there is a desire to reach various segments of society — usually, I contend, three main ones. Although there is some overlap among the three, there are these media: (1) class, (2) mass and (3) crass. The small part (the apex) of the triangle represents the "class" media — the quality or elitist media. Below them, in the midsection of the triangle, is a much larger segment of media — the "mass" media. And at the broad bottom of the triangle are the popular, "crass," or vulgar media. I have adapted this trinary model from Plato's (Book IV, *Republic*) three kinds of lives — the philosophic, the ambitious and the appetitive.

This triad of audience types, based on Plato's classification above, is an attitudinal typology. Members of each audience group are drawn together by a basic attitude toward message content. The "intellectual" audience members (drawn to the class media), for instance, are not necessarily more intelligent than other types of audience members. It is just that they are disposed to want more thoughtful, serious material. The "practical" audience is wider-ranging, having a desire for more utilitarian messages. And the "illiterate" audience is not necessarily functionally illiterate but, rather, attitudinally illiterate. They do not like to read, to think, to analyze, to ponder the more profound aspects of the world around them.

Also it must be said that there are members of each audience who roam among the three types of media. Each category of media — class, mass and crass — express some overlap in their content but not much. And their respective audiences are not pure and static — some are moving up to more serious media; others are moving down to more vapid and popular media. But at any one time the various audiences are predominantly drawn to their favored media.

I

It is rather obvious that the class media would have the smallest audience of the three.

They are aimed at the serious, cultured, well-educated readers, listeners and viewers (Merrill, 1968). They provide intellectual material, ideas, analysis and depth reports, and they stress more esoteric political, economic and cultural subjects. They include elite newspapers (e.g. *The New York Times, Le Monde, Neue Zuercher Zeitung*), magazines (e.g., *National Geographic, Atlantic Monthly*, and *Harper's*), political reviews (e.g. *New Republic* and *National Review*). Certain TV shows (e.g. the history channel) and broadcasting like National Public Radio (NPR), Public Broadcasting System (PBS), and C-Span. Discovery channel's nonfiction show with Ted Koppel that started in early 2006 is a good example of a show catering to serious audiences desiring ideas, analysis, deep background, and culture. The class media try to provide this.

The class media try to go behind the superficiality of people and events they deal with. Journalists working for such media try to get at the "why" of the news — at the causes — and not only the events. They subscribe to the belief that every event has a cause, and every cause is an event. The class media try to get into the minds of the people being reported. They may not go as far as Bishop Berkeley (believing that all that exists are minds and their ideas), but they recognize that ideas are as newsworthy as events. Joseph Epstein (2006), in his thoughtful article in *Commentary*, praises such media for their integrity, impartiality of coverage and the reasoned cogency of their editorial positions. There are a handful of such papers around the world (Merrill, 1968) seeking elite influence and global impact, and appealing to an intellectual audience is not a popular one.

The intellectual audience is one that takes serious things seriously. It enjoys the stimulation afforded by good writing, clear thinking and rational discourse. This does not mean that members of this group never watch a soap opera or find some satisfaction in popular music. But it does mean that they are likely to be the same ones who prefer good wine, classical literature and music, poetry and Broadway plays. Quite simply, they like to think, discuss and seek mental, spiritual and aesthetic pleasures. Theirs is largely a life of the mind.

II

The serious intellectual air of the class media is too rarified for most people. Therefore, the most pervasive and important of the media — at least in a libertarian, capitalist country — are the mass media. They are the providers of practical information, general interest news and features, entertainment (such as comic strips), self-improvement information, a variety of advertisements and sports coverage. This is really the most materialist media segment, and what we usually think of when we speak of the "mass media." The great range of middle-area general newspapers (e.g. *Atlanta Constitution, Kansas City Star, Chicago Tribune*) on through smaller-circulation papers (e.g. *Orlando Sentinel, Denver Post , Shreveport Times*) would certainly be "mass" media.

There is no paucity of information in the mass media. In fact, there is such a variety of material that the consumer has a problem finding news in the vast outpouring. The editor of *Columbia Journalism Review* put it succinctly in 2005 (March/April) when he wrote there is "simply too much noise [in the mass media], that getting straight news from this hyped and opinion-loaded beast feels like trying to drink from a fire hose."

Members of the economic middle-class — and particularly the more affluent ones — comprise the audience of the "mass" media. They want a variety of information and direction — religious, hunting-fishing news, home and garden information, health and education news, and all kinds of material for self-improvement. And they get large doses of it. They are the great consumers of advertising, and, as such, they are the mainstay of the general media. Naturally, in a society having a large middle class with a penchant for entertainment and materialism, one would find the most vibrant mass media system.

Newspapers once thought of as the serious press are fast becoming frivolous. The *Milwaukee Journal*, the *St. Louis Post-Dispatch*, and the *Courier-Journal* of Louisville are good examples. Well, maybe they are not frivolous but certainly they are mundane and increasingly popular. In such papers, scandal and entertainment are replacing what once was "hard news." Spurred on by the success of *USA Today*, the mass media are adopting the principle of making their contents fast-paced, short and entertaining, with color splashed liberally about on the pages.

It seems that less and less does this middle class audience want news. Or at least there seems to be developing a mindset that is satisfied with little news. David Cay Johnston (2005) of *The New York Times* opined in *Columbia Journalism Review* that fewer people are paying attention [to the press], and "more of those who do ... reject all or part of the news." He added that there is "a hostility and suspicion" in the audience that reporters and editors themselves detect.

So the "mass" media are slowly moving away from hard news, providing increasing amounts of feature material, profiles of successful persons and entertainment of all kinds. News, while still important to these media, is succumbing to the practical dalliances of the broad middle classes, increasingly educated but not intellectual in their media tastes. Many mass media today are accused of "dumbing down" their language so as to satisfy more and more of their audience members.

I seriously doubt that this is being done. In the first place, I think mass media writers write as well as they can — producing material that is natural for them. No journalist I have known "dumbs down"; if the writing is concise and simple, that is because that is the way that journalist writes. It would take a brilliant journalist to write at, say, "an eighth-grade level." Content or story-substance, not writing level, may be "dumbed down," and one finds this in many crass or vulgarized media. Considering the broad spectrum of audience members and their various interests, mass media are not doing such a bad job. But no doubt they can improve in both writing quality and substance.

III

The situation can be worse and, as we go lower into the media pyramid we get to the "attitudinal illiterates" that cling to the thoughtless, superficial, entertainment-and-picture-oriented, negative and sensational messages that are being generated by the crass media. These audience members may not really be illiterate, but they expose themselves to TV and movies mainly. Millions of them might be called "attitudinal illiterates." They may be able to read and write, but they do not want to. They are mentally lazy. They care little for serious news and pass most of their days wallowing in the slime of journalism, wading through the dirty gossip, obscene pictures, and titillating writing that is spawned by press practitioners in the crass media.

Many in this audience are poor but not all by any means. In fact, many "illiterates" are from wealthy families. There is an element of alienation and hopelessness about them. They aspire to little beyond their physical appetites. They do not want to think. They want to enjoy in a kind of hedonistic way. And they expose themselves to media that provide this low or crass satisfaction. One might say that the majority of them are hedonistic narcissists, wanting to get through life with as little mental exertion as possible.

One perhaps cannot say that television is itself a "crass medium," but it is safe to say that as an instrument it provides a seemingly insatiable menu of crass programming. The few intellectual programs on TV are like occasional oases in a vast desert of mediocrity and vulgarity. Many (or most) TV shows are examples of "crass" communication. Radio is better but not much. Movies are often "crass," having little or no redeeming social value. Checkout-counter tabloids, mainly pictures of sex and violence, entice millions of "illiterates" every day. And "adult" movies spread their subterranean sludge into the minds of lost souls across the globe, while the Internet provides more word-loving viewers a chance to descend into the netherworld of pornography and superficiality.

Even back at mid-20th century, Richard Weaver (1948, p. vi) wrote that the masses were dominating the American culture, and along with the adulteration of equality and the loss "of those things which are essential to the life of civility and culture," high quality in the media was ever more doubtful. Little wonder that "crass" media are gaining ground and their sordid and shallow messages are even invading the "mass" media. Civility and culture, if in short supply, will naturally be in short supply in the media. Undoubtedly in the future ever more of the population will be siphoned off into the Internet with its diversity of unchecked bloggerism and assorted vulgarity. The media increasingly, with the possible exception of a few elite or class media, slip into nihilistic and thoughtless degeneracy. The sound of the few civil and cultured individuals will truly be voices crying in the wilderness of crass communication.

Class and mass communicators are aware that the great canaille are beyond their reach for they are on the fringes of society, uninvolved in a democratic society. These "illiterate" members of society are largely ignorant, but as Socrates is made to say in Plato's Symposium, they are generally satisfied with themselves. They have no desire to be better informed or to think about the complexities of the world. No doubt that Socrates was right, which means that the class and mass media should not despair that they cannot reach the "appetitive" (Plato) population with solid information and wise analysis.

In concluding this discussion, I should stress again that the three classes of media and audiences above are not static. There is the mass medium that, seeking more exposure, is becoming more popular and appealing increasingly to the intellectually lazy audience. And there is another mass medium that, with different leadership and quality of staff, offers more serious fare and strives for a solid place in the elite or class category. But then there are media of all three types that are content with their basic status: the class media wanting to improve their quality, the mass wanting to reach an enlarged middle class, and the crass media wanting to supply more scandal and sex.

Just as birds of a feather flock together, audiences tend to adhere to agreeable media and messages that give them pleasure. Intellectual pleasure, social and materialistic pleasure, and popular or vulgar pleasure. The distinctive products of the various media stem from the fundamental concepts intrinsic in communication. In accepting certain types of messages, the general public satisfies the tastes of its different segments. Around these segments of media reality has developed a fascinating semantically problematic belief system. This system often obscures the quiddity — the essence — of the concepts being considered.

CHAPTER 5

MYTHOLOGY

A mythology hovers over the media of public communication and their various activities and policies. What we see or think we see is not always what is there. Just what media contribute to society is problematic, certainly not very clear. Their physical presence is obvious; their purpose and social consequences are far less so. As sociologists would put it, the media structure (personnel and equipment/facilities) is much clearer than the concepts (purposes, philosophy, policies, etc.). It is from media concepts principally that myths evolve, swirling with mystic circles and settling with a kind of ephemeral reality on the communication landscape.

Myths help us believe what we cannot understand. They simplify the complex and romanticize the puzzling aspects of life. Myths are, in short, based on the phenomena (as Kant called them) of the world, attempting to translate them into believable pictures in our minds. The media produce and transmit myths. They thus inscribe these believable pictures in our minds, wrapped in often contradictory packages that conceal basic truths. Even the concept that the media create our world is itself a myth. Our real world, or parts of it (*noumena*: Kant again), quite often pushes through the nets of mythology and impacts us directly through our senses. The giant rainmaker in the clouds can, and often does, become nothing more than the cloud.

Nevertheless, the media are powerful communication instruments and this is no myth. Advertising agencies and political promoters can attest to that. Mythmaking in itself is potent. It wraps the human mind around an idea and skitters off with it, trailing truth and error as it goes.

I

Myths contain considerable truth. That's why they are found everywhere and at all times.

And they are also entertaining, soul-satisfying, and psychologically vitalizing. In the field of mass communication they are numerous, weaving in and out of conceptual venues and spinning their webs of pleasant deceit and stimulating endless debates and controversies.

One of the most interesting ones is what I would call the Myth of Professionalism. Many journalists consider themselves professionals and journalism as a profession. But false on both counts. A nice myth, one that attributes to journalism a kind of respect, status, and quality that the older terms "craft" or "trade" are unable to achieve. Again, one of the problems is the semantic problem. But, after all, are not most of our controversial dialogic problems semantic?

To many, being a "professional journalist," for example, simply implies being a hard-working, efficient, quality journalist — doing well the task assumed. To others it means working for a mass medium such as a newspaper or a news radio station — being in the "profession" of journalism. And to others it simply means being a "journalist." This, of course, brings up another semantic problem — just what constitutes a "journalist.?" I see a journalist as one who works for an institutionalized medium in a capacity relating to the getting, writing, editing, and commenting on the news. Certainly "journalist" is easier to define than a "professional journalist."

From a sociological perspective, a profession is not simply a business or a specialized "calling" (e.g. being a theologian or minister). Nor does it separate the good practitioner from the mediocre or bad. A true profession is an institutionalized collection of public service workers who, although individualists, set aside many personal preferences in order to have a collective spirit and a set of self-determined standards to guide their group or profession. These professionals have minimum entrance requirements, a body of moral principles, a system for getting rid of unprofessional members, a sense of collective identity and pride, and a determination to have freedom from outside interference. This, in a broad sense, is a profession. Journalism is presently not one.

The Society of Professional Journalists in the United States in its very title is an example of the perpetuation of this myth. Earlier simply known as Sigma Delta Chi, this organization, holding local, regional and national meetings and publishing a magazine (*The Quill*) is made up of journalists who are called professional. Just what that means, the society does not worry about. Actually it means any journalist. Nobody is asked, upon entering journalism, if he or she is a "professional." But the term sounds good and, like most myths, is not examined for intrinsic meaning. One wonders why the organization is not simply called "The Society of Journalists." That would be semantically troubling enough.

II

A couple of so-called "rights" are interesting myths. Let us look at them briefly. First is the oft-proclaimed "people's right to know." This is a wonderful myth, for there is, of course, no meaningful right to know. There is no constitutional or legal right to know. If there were, it would certainly show up in the Bill of Rights. Journalists like to call on this "right" to try to get information from reticent sources and to justify their publication of certain information. But such a right is pure myth.

If there were such a right, the media would be among the first to complain. For a right to know assumes a responsibility on the part of somebody to fulfill this right. That would mean the media, as well as the government and private institutions, would have to see to it that the people know. Know what? Good question. Perhaps everything, unless one would want to limit the right substantially. If the press, for example, were responsible for letting the people know, would not that violate the press's freedom as granted by the First Amendment? The press, of course, has no such responsibility because the people have no such right.

Now, the people may have a curiosity to know, or even from time to time a need to know. But curiosity and need are not the same as a "right." I work for a TV station and I "need" a car to get to and from work. But I don't have a right to have a car. Like the public or the people out there in Medialand, I may have a need but that does not translate into a right to have a car or knowledge. What I have, and it is self-evident, is a right to try to know. Or to have a car. This right-to-know myth is largely heralded by media people who really don't need to push it. They already have their First Amendment freedom and don't need any people's "right" to justify their actions. But it is another myth that sounds good and tends to place the media in sync with the broad concept of democracy.

Another "right" is often proclaimed: the right of public access to the media. This is an interesting myth for it is in conflict with the very concept of capitalism and private property so important to the British philosopher John Locke and the American Founding Fathers. The press is a private institution (business) in the United States and the publisher and/or the stockholders, like proprietors of any business, select the product to be sold.

It may be a socially responsible act to permit citizens to express their opinions and inject their news items into the newspaper, for instance, but there is no "right of access" for the citizens. A good publisher or editor will want to have some representation, for circulation if for no other reason, but this will be purely voluntary — and to a large extent selfishly motivated — and not to fulfill some "people's right." But the shift appears to be from the press's freedom to control content to the people's freedom of access.

This idea has a long history in the United States. Back in 1969, Jerome Barron, a law professor at George Washington University, advocated public access to the media and even called it a "new First Amendment right." Reeking of a kind of semantic revisionism spawned by postmodernism, he believed all minority opinions and "unpopular" points of view should be legally admitted to the press.

This idea was lauded by the ACLU and was popular up through the 1980s when it began to fade out. Harvard's Zechariah Chafee saw it as untenable and dangerous. Press critic Ben Bagdikian agreed, saying that news judgment must be made by the journalists themselves. Others, like John Hohenberg, professor of journalism at Columbia University at the time, endorsed Barron's idea, deploring the lack of public access to the media.

An early pioneer in anti-liberal ideas about freedom was Joseph de Maistre (1753-1821), a French-speaking lawyer and philosopher from Savoy, who poured scorn on Enlightenment thinking and the French Revolution. He especially saw the freedom-loving spirit that was rising as a danger and felt the world was heading toward chaos. He argued his conservative philosophy with a writing style and humor probably unmatched by any other writer of the time. Like today's communitarians, Maistre contended that liberal ideas were to blame for the low state of Western society. Unlike the communitarians, he was an extremist and an authoritarian. What was needed was not press autonomy and self-determination but order and security. Maistre's arsenal of weapons against Enlightenment liberalism, in many ways reflecting the arguments of Thrasymachus in his famous dialog with Socrates, was among the most effective ever assembled (Holmes).

It should be noted, however, that Maistre's concept of people's rights was quite distinct from Barron's. The Frenchman, agreeing with Thrasymachus that might makes right, would be perfectly satisfied with editorial decisions being totally in the hands of the editor or publisher. Barron, on the other hand, would democratize might, placing it more in the hands of the public. He would revise Maistre by saying that democratic might makes right.

Reminicient of Maistre (who with Edmund Burke founded European conservatism) was a Russian-American who provided America with an anti-liberal philosophy that had a great appeal in America in the 20th century. Ayn Rand, one of the century's foremost (at least, most popular) writers took great exception to Barron's idea of people's journalism. She said that the right of free speech means that a person has a right to express ideas without danger of interference from government. But it does not mean, she emphasizes, that others must provide this person with a radio station or a printing press through which to express these ideas. For her, a right of public access is a myth. She was instrumental in spreading European conservativism to the United States, although it was a more individualistic brand than that strict authoritarianism of Maistre.

In spite of critics like Rand and Harvard's Chafee, the idea of a right of public access has held on in some circles. The defenders say that press self-determination is bad because not everybody and every group gets equal access to the press. Friedrich Hayek in his Road to Serfdom counters this by saying that as long as dissent is not suppressed, important ideas will always be available in a society and will be tested by argument and propaganda. It is not necessary that every single person participate in the process. Hayek's position seems to me to be beyond rational criticism.

Although the old right-of-access myth had somewhat dissipated by the 21st century, its democratically oriented foundation is still with us. But as the Internet becomes ever more popular and people are radically empowered to express themselves, the issue may remain dormant for some time. Media access may still be difficult for the public, but communication access is ever more possible.

The whole subject of "rights" may well be nothing but myth. Where do we get rights, even so-called "human rights"? It seems to me that we come into the world without rights, and we leave the world without rights. The only right I might have is the right to think I have rights.

III

An important myth of modern communication could be called the Myth of the Newspaper. Contrary to popular usage, no newspapers exist in the United States or perhaps in the whole world. We have "papers" aplenty; the globe is filled with various kinds of sheets, potpourri journals, specialized letters and publications of all kinds — but no newspapers. My students and I, for many years, have conducted content analyses of various so-called newspapers and we have found that "news" accounts for around 10% of the average paper's content.

Yet these sheets are called "NEWSpapers."

Without getting too specific, let us look at this average or typical paper. Right off the top there is advertising — taking up some 55% - 65% of the total space. Then there are the editorials, columns, letters to the editor, op-ed page commentaries. And puzzles, and in some papers, comic strips. And then there are the profiles and feature stories, and non-news pictures consuming another big block of space. We are left with about 10% (perhaps slightly more) for what most editors and readers would call news. A cautionary note should be injected here: In our studies we did not count sports stories as news, although many people would. We consider sports news as entertainment — if news at all, then what is known as "soft news."

Even with sports material counted in as news, the percentage of space would increase only by some 5%, meaning that a typical paper gives only some 15% of its space to news. Newspaper is really a misnomer — a myth proclaiming that if you buy the paper, you get the news. Far from it.

"News," as has been pointed out earlier, is one of the most difficult — if not the most difficult — semantic problems in journalism. Just what is meant by the term "news"? Although it is at the very heart of journalism, nobody seems to know what it means. Or, said another way, everybody seems to know what it is. News is made in the journalist's brain and can be anything a particular journalist wants to consider news — from a bird falling from a tree to a powerful explosion in Iraq.

What's news? The question is heard often. A reply: Mrs. Brown has a bad cold. Another: John Doe died yesterday in a car crash. Textbook definitions and prerequisites for news don't count for much, although such basics as proximity, magnitude, prominence are self-evident. For many editors, the President breaking his arm is big news, while the breaking of my neck is not news at all. Relativity is the name of the news game and it is played constantly without any rules. Decision-making subjectivity is another name, and it determines that journalism is actually a subjective, unscientific, personal and biased enterprise. William Hachten (1987) of the University of Wisconsin has rightfully called it a "news prism." Little wonder that so many journalists fall into the pit of confusion and uncertainty.

But having said that, we must admit that there is a kind of core meaning for the news. It is generally believed that it must include factual information, devoid of the reporter's own overt opinion. The avowed purpose of news is to inform, to give the salient aspects of a story, and to be credible. It is not principally to entertain, to inspire, to titillate, to interpret, to persuade, or to motivate. It is to inform. Therefore, the content analysis of newspapers mentioned earlier is not entirely meaningless. Most journalists seem to have a fairly consistent idea of news, although there can be wide variation. At least there is an understanding of what is not news — e.g. advertising, editorials, feature stories, letters, essays, puzzles, and comics and other entertainment pieces. So, in spite of semantic difficulties, we can be safe in saying that what is left (the "news") takes up very little space in a "newspaper."

Another myth that has great lasting power is that a pluralism of media in a community provides more news and perspectives than only one or a very few. If, for example, Mozell, Arkansas, has two newspapers, two radio stations, and a TV station, the people of Mozell have access to more news than do the people of Astam, New Mexico. Astam has only one newspaper and one radio station. The Mozell people are at an advantage. This is common wisdom. But it is a myth.

Quantity and diversity of news and opinion is dependent on more than the number of media or outlets in a community. Mozell's five media may be small, ill-run, with small staffs and executives not interested in editorial quality. On the other hand Astam's two media may be vigorous, enterprising, with well-paid staffs and executives interested in providing the community with as much information as possible. An analysis of the media in the two communities may well find that fewer is better, that the people of Astam have access to a greater variety and quality of information than those living in Mozell.

What is important for a well-informed citizenry is not the number of media available, but the quality and amount of news and other information available. Of course, other factors also enter in here — such as the audience's interest in being informed and the amount of available information they expose themselves to. But these factors are beyond the control of the media.

Today many press critics gather their statistics about mergers, group ownerships, chains and the like, and despair of the state of journalism. Big fish are eating the little fish, and the assumption is that we need the little fish. Again they are confusing "unit" pluralism (number of media) with "subject-matter pluralism." Unit pluralism does not assure an informed public. It is quite possible that one big media conglomerate like Gannett can have a newspaper in a city that can provide more news than several smaller privately owned newspapers. This is not to say that it does provide more news.

Really the only way to get at a meaningful pluralism (message pluralism) is to conduct thorough, and continuing, content analyses. The stress must be on content, not on numbers of media or ownerships. The myth persists however that we have a shrinkage of the number of media and ownerships in the United States and, therefore, citizens are being less well informed. It may be so, but it may not. Quite often a big newspaper can, because of bigger staff and facilities, provide a greater range of information than can several small papers with poorly paid and overworked staff. However, no research has been done to shed light on this question. So, another myth.

CHAPTER 6

FREE PRESS AND BLOGGERS

P robably the most enduring myth of the American republic is that we have a free press. After all, the U.S. Constitution itself (in the First Amendment) guarantees that Congress will make no laws abridging freedom of the press. And the country has a long tradition of freedom of expression stretching from the British and French Enlightenment liberalism. Surely we have a free press. Or do we?

First, we must note the problem with the First Amendment free press clause. "Congress" shall make no law abridging the freedom of the press. Let's assume that Congress has not passed such laws, we must ask these questions: What about the Judicial Branch? What about the Executive Branch? A student of history can find many instances where the Supreme Court, through its rules, has narrowed the scope of press freedom, and lower courts have jailed journalists for one reason or another. And the President and his governmental branch (including the military establishment) have often, through executive orders, denied access to the press, censored the press, and kept the press at bay (e.g. in the Grenada invasion toward the end of the 20th century).

So even from a legal standpoint vis-à-vis government, the American press is not free. This does not mean, of course, that it does not have a considerable degree of freedom. It always comes out very high in the annual Freedom House's hierarchy of international press freedom. Many questions arise about press freedom. Let us look at three: (1) Does press freedom belong to the people or to the press? (2) Does press freedom imply some kind of responsibility and, if so, what kind of responsibility? (3) What exactly are the limits to press freedom, if there are any? Let me give my answers to these questions very briefly. Press freedom belongs to the press, not the people. Many disagree with this, but "the people" have freedom of speech; the press has freedom of the press. Secondly, press freedom obviously implies some kind of responsibility on the part of the press. Just what this is, however, is problematic. Libel laws (contrary to First Amendment?), for instance, indicate one type of responsibility. Self-censorship (or other) during time of war or national emergency indicates another type. Limits to press freedom? Yes, but only those the press sets for itself.

I

Theoretically, one of the advantages of an Enlightenment-instituted free press is that market forces will automatically hold the press responsible (accountable) for its action. This has been denied by many scholars, especially in the late 20th century. Claude-Jean Bertrand (2003) insists that media in many countries are not giving the public information that it needs, nor are they providing a forum for discussion, nor transmitting culture, nor entertaining the people. Market forces, he says, will not assure accountability.

Bertrand, a French scholar, proposes an accountability system that would pressure media managers to be accountable. Part of the system would be the use of codes of ethics, press councils, ombudsmen, journalism reviews and education, all of which have been tried. Bertrand certainly is not suggesting in any way that government force the media to be accountable. In spite of his accountability mechanisms, he insists that he has not deserted the libertarian emphasis of the Enlightenment.

The libertarian ideas of the 18th and early 19th centuries evolved into Romanticism and then, in the 20th century, into Existentialism. Freedom of expression and individualism seemed to be enthroned. In Germany, for example, philosophers like Johan G. Fichte were stressing self-determination, even under tyrannical regimes. Such self-determination was freedom, for as Fichte said, the inner self can always be free. And the idea was pushed that self-control was not control; in fact, one is free to make oneself a slave. The stress here was on the inner life. This view is a long way from the great foe of inner freedom — fatalism, that puts some kind of transcendental controller in charge of a person's life.

The British and French ideas about freedom, however, were more down to earth. Freedom meant basically freedom from the iron hand of the State, an idea that spread to the American colonies in the form of press autonomy or editorial determination. Among the leaders in this libertarian movement were the British natural rights philosophers John Locke and Herbert Spencer. Freedom should be maximized, said Spencer, and every person should be free to do as he or she wishes as long as such action does not infringe on the equal freedom of another person. This was pretty much the common belief of the Enlightenment and for years later in the Western world. In the 1950s, for example, the philosopher Karl Popper was extolling freedom and democracy and warning against the heritage of Plato which he saw as leading to a regimented society.

It was about mid-20th-century, while Popper was issuing his warning, that many scholars began criticizing press freedom or libertarianism (of the Enlightenment variety) as harmful to society. A strong reaction set in against libertarianism, led largely by the critical theorists, whose main target was capitalism. The new emphasis shifted to society, to egalitarianism, to democratizing the press, to eliminating the negative tendencies of the hierarchical media structure and the growth of big conglomerates and powerful media managers.

An interesting thing about freedom is that it includes the freedom to be led, to be controlled, to be directed, to be limited, or even curtailed. This idea stems from Plato's famous "paradox of freedom," which asserts that a free people (or a majority of them) may say they do not want to rule and would like to give up their freedom to a tyrant. One might refer to this as democratic authoritarianism.

Normally workers for a newspaper, for example, may want to be led by an editor or publisher. They use their freedom to acquiesce in their subservient roles, to follow not lead, to obey not command. And even when we think of the media executives as the leaders, hopes are that they will be the "wisest," not necessarily the "best" persons for their jobs. This opens the possibility that "wise" editors, for instance, may use their wisdom to decide to step aside and let the "best" have more authority. Then the best leaders may in turn decide to expand "public journalism" so as to permit more poorly qualified non-journalists to become decision-makers.

A basic assumption is that freedom is necessary but needs to be used responsibly. We hear such statements so often it is almost accepted as a given. But I would postulate that freedom is, indeed, not a given — at least a positive given. Why not say that control is necessary but needs to be injected with shots of freedom? If a newspaper publisher provides control but with some room for free will by the staff, then I would not have the Civil Liberties Union pounce upon him. In fact, it seems that today with Enlightenment liberalism under attack and social harmony and stability encouraged, control or restrained media would be favorably accepted by responsible journalists. It may take increased control to stop this Hobbsian war of all against all and reach a Platonic level of wise media direction.

II

Although the Platonic ideal of the wise leader, the philosopher king, generally has appeal for intellectuals, there are signs today that the view is not able to emerge from the shadows of democracy and egalitarianism. For example, Amitai Etzioni, an American sociologist, popularized what was called communitarianism. And the Pew Foundation — along with communication scholars like Ted Glasser, James Carey, Howard Zinn, and Robert McChesney, who are imbued with an early Marxian concern for egalitarian democracy — have supported what they called "public" or "civic" journalism. This is an attempt to bring the public into the decision-making of the media, to increase democratization. This public journalism has never really enjoyed wide approval in practical journalism, although it made some waves at the end of the last century. And it is still around. Most newspapers did change some of their operations to permit more citizen participation, but by the end of the new century's first decade public journalism was still struggling for greater support.

In the intellectual world — contrary to the world of the media — the ideas behind communitarianism have continued to make headway. The public, not the press, should have the freedom: This is a communitarian mantra. The German philosopher Jürgen Habermas and many British, Canadian, and American academics are emphasizing more interactive and participatory communication. James Carey of Columbia talks of "society conversing" and Clifford Christians of Illinois refers to "public conversation." Habermas would like to see society return to the old English coffee house dialogues of the days of Addison and Steele. The whole idea of networking, participation, and honest communication among interested, informed, and articulate individuals has been moderately successful. But it involves just a handful of people, with the great masses left on the outside.

Christians, a leader in journalistic communitarianism, notes (Land and Hornaday, 2006, p. 62) that social systems encapsulate individuals at birth, retain them through life, and endure after them. Therefore, Christians believes that community is a prerequisite for ethical action. He further stresses the importance of "humans-in-relation," thereby reorients selfhood but does not reject it. Christians believes (p.65) that Enlightenment liberals, with their emphasis on individual freedom, ignores or minimizes the relationship among members of the community. And communitarians see this as a weakness of liberal philosophy steeped as it is in J. S. Mill's untilitarianism.

The avowed purpose behind this trend toward communitarianism and democratization is to enlarge the public sphere of discourse, to make it possible for members of society to converse. Freedom of communication is thereby spread over a wider segment of the public, and traditional press freedom is drained from the elitists who rule the traditional media. Increasingly the talk is of the "people's freedom," not the press's freedom. For the communitarians, freedom must be sacrificed to public interaction, stability and order.

Friedrich Hayek (1944, p. 222) noted that small communities will provide common views on projected tasks and values, and when a community disappears, force and coercion take its place. Futurist Francis Fukuyama adds his voice to a communitarian emphasis (1999, p. 59), by pointing out that loss of the spirit of community results in "the great disruption" in society

In spite of the growing popularity of community, the spirit of the Enlightenment is not dead. Nor is the elitist spirit of Plato. Media people (at least those at the top) still think of vertical authority and insist on freedom to do pretty much what they desire. They think they are free, but public opinion, advertisers, boards of directors and the ever-present Government exert great pressures on them. For them, democratic communication is on the back burner and press freedom, at least idealistic rhetoric about it, is still much alive. In spite of its vagueness and unused potential, it is a popular free-market mantra, a kind of rallying myth trailing red-white-and blue streamers behind it.

The critical theorists and communitarians of the 20th century have not been alone to point out the basic weaknesses of the American press. Just before mid-19th century the Frenchman Alexis de Tocqueville (*Democracy in America*) was perhaps the first to note the early American press's vulgar appeals to passions and its negative social impact. About a century later the Hutchins Commission made a similar indictment. And since the 1950s the critical theorists, communitarians and public journalists have further scored the American media for their profit-making incentives and their arrogance and have claimed that the press was too much concerned with freedom and too little concerned with their public responsibility.

Tocqueville, while critical of the media establishment, was also warning Americans of what might result from too much democracy. He even suggested, anticipating the thoughts of Erich Fromm (1941) later on, that the people probably do not want to shape their own destinies. A deep desire for intellectual paternalism and a basic laziness seem to keep people from venturing into the traumatic realm of journalistic participation. It could be, however, that the new electronic media will lead to more public expression. More positive (utililized) freedom, perhaps, but freedom is a fragile thing.

II

The sharks of authoritarianism are hungry. They are constantly eating away at the concept of freedom. Autocratic news directors and publishers, advertisers, lawyers in the newsroom, arrogant reporters, political and religious factions, greater concern for profits, court mandates, codes of ethics — all of these and more — are pressuring and diminishing journalistic autonomy. And, of course, in dictatorial countries, the political authority is continuing its direct control of the media.

Plato and his long list of successors (both wise and unwise) evidence little faith in the people and their ability to be free and unstructured. What is needed, say many, is some version of Hobbes' Leviathan or a regime of Papal Power envisioned by Joseph deMaistre. Social engineering is not a thing of the past, and the media fall prey to the arguments for stability and security trumping the assumed benefits of freedom. And even though the ideals of libertarianism and existentialism find a prominent place in some of our public media, the attraction of a centralized authority finds widespread popularity throughout the world. If libertarianism will not compromise with authority, then the forces of order and control will continue to press their case and call for more responsibility.

As British philosopher R. H. S. Crossman has put it (Thorson, 1963, p. 39), the perfect State (accepting Plato's highly regimented society) will be for the average person "a fool's paradise," controlled by a few wise people, "who out of their compassion for the masses provide them with superstitions and ceremonies and popular philosophies fit for their feeble capacities." Crossman (p. 40) is harshly critical of Platonic authoritarianism, calling it the most savage attack on liberal ideas in history, and Plato's perfect state" not a democracy of equals but an aristocracy in which "cultured gentlemen care with paternal solicitude for the toiling masses."

From the ancient warrior chieftains to the medieval Church authorities to the royal, plutocratic and socialistic leaders of today, this Platonic spirit of social control and order is still a potent force. One writer, Roderick Seidenberg (1974), has noted the steady drift toward social control and order. He says (p. 207) that this trend toward solidarity and order has all but destroyed the world of Enlightenment individualism, not as by "a wind in the treetops, but at its roots by an earthquake!" He called it (p. 113) a "shifting social paradigm of emerging historical determinism," where the individual is gradually converted into a "frictionless member of the community."

As I understand it, a society or community run by the profit motive is not really what the communitarians want. Their vision is collective democratic decision-making, where nonmaterial considerations bring about common values and a desire to work together for the good of all. In spite of this idealized desire, I think it must be said that communitarians are in favor of an ordered society, but with the order of community replacing the disorder coming out of Enlightenment individualism. Pressure to conform, yes, but this would be the pressure of the whole on the one — the community on the individual.

I think it should be stressed that communities are not necessarily good. A community of lawless gang members, democratically composed, is not good. The democratic "community" of Germans (minus the Jews) just before and during World War II was not good. And then there is the nondemocratic community of Singapore. Good. And democratic Zimbabwe and post-apartheid South Africa. Not good. And post-Franco democratic Spain. Good. And the 2006 election to power of the terrorist Hamas party in Palestine. Not good.

A community may be socially good (progressive) or bad (regressive), irrespective of its degree of democracy. The desire for order, stability and security is not attached to a single modern political label; communitarians are found across the political spectrum. Public media, likewise, can be autocratic and good; they can be democratic and bad. One must look beyond the labels to the essence of the government or of the public medium. As the American press democratizes (more voices in communication), does this mean that it will result in a better country or a worse country? There is much to worry about.

III

In the United States, the institutionalized media, clinging to their vertical authority, are becoming increasingly worried about a counter-position in communication: the bloggers. And well they might be. Bloggers are democratizing communication and are drawing great audiences away from basic media messages. People are, as the communitarians hope for, talking more and more with each other and listening to standard messages less and less. Internet blogging has been called "journalism's backseat drivers" (Barb Palser) that offers critiques of the news media and myriads of perspectives and accounts of the news

"Individualism and pluralism" is the name of the game for the new "journalists" of the Internet. Feisty and energetic, bloggers are thrusting themselves into the world of journalism, many of them actually considering themselves journalists. Many bloggers think the mainstream media untrustworthy, lazy and self-righteous, institutions that need watching carefully. Bloggers think they can do this watching. They see themselves as publishing their own little news-opinion papers. Perhaps they see themselves as the "fifth estate," keeping a watch on the institutionalized media as well as on government.

People talking on the telephone are communicators, but they are not journalists. These may be "phonies," but they are not journalists. And I resent the idea that bloggers are journalists. They certainly can be called public communicators, but not journalists. If bloggers are journalists, then those in journalism education should go out of business, for anyone and everyone is a journalist. All that is necessary for journalism then are computer skills. Is the blogger protected by the "free press" clause of the First Amendment? Certainly the bloggers do supplement journalism, just as a thousand other communication activities do.

As Barb Palser points out in *American Journalism Review*, bloggers go beyond exposing weaknesses in journalism. They serve the media as sources of information and as public opinion channels. (Government information services do the same.) People in the blogging business, of course, have their many and inherent weaknesses. But they have extended the existentialist spirit into public communication. Stressing freedom, individualism and action, they have injected a new spirit of verve and vigor into the public sphere. They have done much that the public or civic journalists have been calling for: involvement of many more people in the public conversation. No longer do the mainstream media have a monopoly on fact and opinion.

So we can see this democratizing communication, in spite of enlarging public conversation, is taking us in a more specialized direction. Bloggers, unlike the regular media, can throw their spotlights on esoteric and unusual topics. A blogger can dig deeper and longer into a story than can the conventional media. Having few or no advertisers, the blogger-reporter has no urge to pull his or her punches, writes Richard Posner of *The New York Times*. The writers on the Internet have more freedom than do their counterparts in the media. They may not be called part of the press yet, but they have a kind of grassroots freedom unheard of by the hierarchical mainstream media reporters. This increased freedom, of course, mandates more personal accountability — one of the most problematic issues for anyone in the field of "bloggerism."

At the heart of public communication — for the mainstream journalist or for the blogger — is a sense of ethics, of responsible behavior, of high standards and public service. Even more than in the past, ethical standards veer in the direction of the individual person. Personal integrity is paramount, increased freedom notwithstanding. Of course there will be bloggers who are irresponsible, careless, biased, inaccurate and superficial. In short, message pluralism will increase and the old Miltonic principle (the truth will win out) will get new life or challenge. More to choose from: the principle of increased diversity. Whether this will help the average citizen find the truth in all this material, perhaps containing little or no truth, is another question.

The bloggers have many advantages over the mainstream media and can flood a vast assortment of information and opinion across the land. But this does not mean that their splintered versions will get much attention. Quite likely the bloggers will not give much attention to global news and will focus on entertainment, on scandals, crime, violence, celebrities and politicians — much like the mainstream media. But, in addition, they will focus on their own personal opinions.

Like the media, bloggers will give people what they themselves are interested in and will not stress the idealized "thirst for knowledge" called for by the small class of intellectuals. As Posner has written, news coverage is "oriented to a public that enjoys competitive sports, not to one that is civic-minded." But with hundreds or thousands of these bloggers and their input, one can hope that some or many of them will report carefully about serious matters and offer sophisticated analysis and opinion. If they are truly existential communicators, they will. If they are complacent, passive and irresponsible, they will do little to improve public communication. In fact, they may speed up the tendency toward entropy.

Finally, blogging can portend a bright future, especially for freedom of expression and message pluralism. Certainly bloggers can go beyond their media brothers and sisters in self-expression. This may or may not be a healthy development, and time will tell if this democratizing of expression will benefit or harm society. For those libertarians who want little or no "gatekeeping" by news directors and editors, the advent of Internet communication appears to be an opening to a bright future. We will see.

CHAPTER 7

CHASING THE SYNTHESIS

In Western media systems, freedom, however mythical in reality, is often seen as the grand objective. All kinds of rationales for freedom have existed, from Herbert Spencer's social Darwinian principle (that if freedom prevails, the weak would be weeded out, leaving only the strong) to John Locke's idea that freedom is a "natural right" (with which everyone is born) to Milton's view of freedom as a "self-righting" process, necessary for the truth to win out in competition with falsehood.

From the 17th century on, freedom has been the big Thesis (dominant paradigm) in Hegel's dialectic. It has been challenged by political Hegelians of the right (fascists) and the left (communists) who have seen the state and a strong authority as preferable to freedom. From Rousseau and Maistre to Hitler, Mussolini, Mao and Stalin, reflecting basic social beliefs of Hegel, the Antithesis has developed. And this antithesis of the dialectic — groupism, stability and order — is becoming well-entrenched despite continued Western genuflection to freedom. Social regimentation or autocratic social structuralism is not necessarily "amoral" (Popper in Thorson, 1963, p. 65), but "is the morality of the closed society — or the group, or of the tribe." According to Popper, it "is not individual selfishness, but it is collective selfishness." And, further referring to Platonic philosophy, Popper notes (p. 63) that "morality is utilitarian — collective utilitarianism — and is no more than political hygiene."

It could be that Aristotle was right: the masses are naturally slaves and, when freed, do not have the moral and intellectual means to face their responsibility. They look for new chains when freed from other chains. And it may be that Thomas Hobbes also was right: People seek neither freedom nor happiness — not even justice — but, above all, security.

Media people, however, assert that they want freedom. And there are those, like Montesquieu (strange talk from a liberal?) who talks of liberty not as doing what we want, but what we "ought" to do. The British philosopher Isaiah Berlin (1977, pp.147-48) points out that Kant agrees with Montesquieu, and even Edmund Burke believed that the individual, for his own good, has a right to be contrained. It is doubtful that many of the media leaders today would agree with such opinion.

Media institutions are strong — especially in their collective sense. They are still holding tenaciously to their freedom where they have it. They see the struggle for freedom as a constant one, fought in the face of a dark future of conformity and self-sacrifice. They see things changing, their freedom being questioned, and they dig in their heels. Libertarians, still harnessed to Enlightenment liberalism (the thesis), bemoan this shift away from freedom brought on by workings of the dialectic.

The synthesis (devoid of extreme authoritarian elements) coming out of this clash of freedom and responsibility seems to be communitarianism (widespread participation in intra-public "conversation") and is seeping deeper into mass communication clothed as civic journalism, democratization and professionalization.

It seems that basic biases underlie communitarianism. Among them is the idea of giving priority to the marginalized and emphasizing the suffering portions of our society (Craig, 2003). This amounts to media bias, but for communitarians it is one that is justified by a moral imperative. As David Craig writes (p. 807), "This ethic of concern draws attention to the importance of the circumstances of the lives of individuals in prompting a depth of concern for them." Christians, Ferre and Fackler (1993, p. 93) have said much the same thing: that media "nurtured by communitarian ethics" must do more than give fair treatment to the events covered; they must recognize "that justice itself — and not merely haphazard public enlightenment" — is what is required. In other words: being just is more important than enlightening the public. Would this not turn the journalist from a reporter into a social worker?

This is a basic question. Does a journalist's concept of virtue override his or her purposeful attempt to be even-handed and as objective as possible? It is a question that communitarians will have to wrestle with for a long time.

I

The Hegelian principle of the person losing self in the state is now being applied to a person's losing self in the society or community, Such a shift in terminology, at least, rids earlier Hegelianism of its negative political implications and stays within the limits of democracy.

Such a shift calls on the American media to give up some of their power gained and retained through their almost total hold on freedom. The synthesis in the dialectic now asks them to share it, to think more of the community than themselves, and to develop a stance that will mitigate their freedom while enlarging their social responsibility and public-involvement in the media.

The Hegelian dialectic is at work in many aspects of public communication. It can be seen in the basic foundational work of journalism — reporting. In the 21st century journalists are recognizing that "objective" news reporting, the mere collections of unbiased information, is unreasonable and does not assure truth-telling. Postmodernism has thrust point-of-view reporting against this former naïve realism and has resulted in the belief that interpretation is inextricably tied up with reality. As Mitchell Stephens ("We're all postmodern now," *Columbia Journalism Review*, July/Aug, 2005, p. 62) has written, "Call it perspective; call it analysis. But what has happened is that modern reporters have had to relearn to scratch their heads, rub their chins, and weigh in. The old line between fact and interpretation has become more difficult to draw." The antinomies have clashed, and a new synthesis is born.

American public communicators, especially journalists dealing with serious ideology, are two-valued (see Korzybski's general semantics) in their basic mindset. They, like their fellow citizens, see things as either-or, black-white, with few if any shades of gray in between. So, just as they see freedom as separate from constraint or control, they see many of their concepts in the same two-valued way.

What is needed is a kind of synthesis — a concern for the middle-way, for the broad range of possibilities that exist toward the midpoint in the either-or spectrum. Korzybski, the ex-Polish count, called this a "multi-valued orientation"; for Hegel it would result in the synthesis of the dialectic — what results when the antithesis clashes with the thesis. Of course, Aristotle had presaged this thinking with his "Golden Mean" — the avoidance of the extremes — as did several of the ancient Chinese sages.

This retreat from extremes is an attempt to treat reality, and the communication of it, in a more scientific way. It is in the same family of linguistic concern as eliminating stereotypes, tying events and ideas to a particular time, and recognizing that entities and ideas are constantly changing. Communication, of course, is really incapable of resolving fully these problems that have been a special concern of the general semanticists and the deconstructionists. Especially troublesome is that people, places and things are constantly changing, always becoming (Heraclitus, 6th century B.C.) something new. In fact, as Nietzsche maintained, we cannot talk about "being" since everything is "becoming." Journalism tends to stultify or present unchanging or rigid images. For example, the media are prone to provide a static, one-dimensional view of a person or place regardless of various changes that have taken place.

This journalistic mindset is devoid of the concept of flux, described from both sides of the world by Heraclitus and Chuang-tzu centuries ago. Or, for that matter, it is really lacking in attention to Hegel's dialectic, to which we shall return now.

Conceptual clashes are common in today's communication landscape. Individualism and collectivism; capitalism and socialism; freedom and authority; scientism and emotion; absolutism and relativism; existentialism and rationalism; subjectivity and objectivity; poetry and prose; journalism and literature; science and art; libertarianism and authoritarianism; conservatism and liberalism. Thinking in opposites basically denies change and complexity. And there are antinomies aplenty to keep our journalism simplistic and stultified.

II

Let us briefly consider two of these dialectical opponents here for they are of vital importance to the public communicator. They are (1) freedom versus authority and (2) subjectivity versus objectivity.

Freedom is closely related to existentialism and authority is closely related to rationalism. And subjectivity is closely related to freedom and existentialism, and objectivity is closely related to rationalism and authority. So one can see that these two sets of antinomies are intertwined in meaning. In a sense, then, we are really looking at two opposing tendencies in communication — subjectivism versus objectivism. It is a consideration of the involved communicator and its opposite, the aloof or neutral communicator.

Friedrich Nietzsche has called these two tendencies or stances the "Dionysian" and the "Apollonian" — the first, the emotionally oriented, and the second, the cerebrally oriented. Here we have antinomies (opposites) that encompass freedom, authority, subjectivity and objectivity, and it is a good way to talk about journalists and journalism.

The Dionysian journalist, named by Nietzsche for the Greek god, Dionysus, would be passionate, sensitive and subjective, akin to the artistic or literary communicator. The Apollonian journalist, named for the Greek god, Apollo, would be more neutral, more objective, more prosaic and more dispassionate, more akin to the scientist.

The basic difference in the two comes from their different basic orientations — the Dionysian has an open or flexible style, whereas the Apollonian has a predictable, closed, or mechanistic style. The existentialist personifies the first, open stance, and the scientifically oriented objectivist, the second or closed stance. The existentialist delights in giving journalism a stamp of individuality, placing great importance on commitment, self-expression and freedom. The objectivist, with prosaic mindset, considers the objective as identical with the factual and is dedicated to facts and devoid of any expression or feeling.

But the pure objectivist, who is still with us here and there, is fading away in this period of postmodernism with its stress on uncertainty and pluralism of interpretations. The reporter becomes part of the story in this new concept; subjectivity is redefined as objectivity. This new formulation, of course, is in its own way just as extremist as its objectivist antinomy. It is a concept that easily slides into opinionated permissiveness where facts are lost in the reporter's spin.

The synthesis here is difficult. How does the reporter retain respect for factual, for impartial, for neutral reporting and at the same time the value of personal perspectives, opinions and feelings? What the reporter can do is to recognize the value of both antinomies — and the weaknesses of both. Needed is C. P. Snow's scientist and artist, Nietzsche's Apollonian and Dionysian. Some of both, but not too much of either, as Aristotle would say. Needed is the recognition that the subjective structuring of and sensitive emphasis on facts will make a neutral and cold story more realistic and truthful.

Here we see the theoretical antinomies stressed by Nietzsche. They are the extreme polar positions, clashing and merging in a continuous battle for dominance in journalism. Beginning in the 20th century, what became the thesis (the objective Apollonian) was soon confronted by its antithesis, the Dionysian (the subjective postmodernist). The dialectic at work. A new synthesis is forming, combining aspects of the former thesis and its antithesis. I have called (1989) this new merger the Apollonysian synthesis. This synthesis is the new developing thesis. In time, no doubt, a new antithesis will attack it and it will morph into another synthesis ... and on and on.

Related to freedom there are other ways to isolate a dialectic. For example, there is the classic clash (Plato, *Republic*, Book I) in the fifth century B.C. of the ideas of Socrates and Callicles. The first regards freedom as service to God and to other people, and the second sees freedom as satisfying personal desires and acting without restraint. Callicles sees freedom as an end in itself; Socrates, on the other hand, envisions freedom as a way to serve justice and the common good. His basic stance was taken up by J. S. Mill in England centuries later. Callicles personifies the extreme existentialist position that those who truly exist (live) should permit emotions and personal desires to flourish and that those who enthrone distributive justice and temperance are nothing but cowards.

Here we have Socratic humanism clashing with Calliclean hedonism and egoism. Socrates notes that it is impossible to satisfy our desires and this indicates the absurdity of the attempt. He also says that those who follow Callicles cannot be really happy; there must be some rational way to differentiate good pleasures from bad. The Socratic position is that freedom is not the pursuit of personal desires but is a disciplined lifestyle that perfects that which is distinctly human — including a concern for other people. Callicles throws his antithesis against Socrates, saying that freedom includes the right to do what others might think is irresponsible. Freedom means freedom, not duty to some utilitarian cause. In this he sounds much like John Locke, with his insistence that freedom is a natural right, not based on the telos of bringing some predetermined consequences.

This dialectical issue has intrigued and frustrated communicators down through the ages. And it is still with us. There are the realists, the men of the world, who run communications media. They believe in Callicles' natural morality and have no qualms about pushing weaker persons aside. They are the superior men, the elite men who believe that might makes right. The Socratic media leader, on the other hand, sees such Callicleans as unhappy and unfree, simply slaves to their passions. Freedom, for the Socratic media person, is not the pursuit of personal pleasure but consists of a disciplined, orderly life that keeps the humanity of others constantly in mind. So as these two perspectives clash, the dialectic synthesis is developing. Mainly its development is due to the intrusion of judiciary insistence on more moderate personal action, but it is still a most problematic issue facing the world of mass communication.

III

Most media workers desire to be happy, whatever else they want. Hedonism has always been a primary philosophical objective. Aristotle, as did Socrates, stressed character-development, being virtuous as opposed to simply following rules. And for Aristotle, virtue is rational activity. When people are not rational, they are not virtuous. Aristotle's rational person is happy, and a happy person is virtuous. His happiness was not what we mean when we say we "feel happy." His concept of happiness is what we mean by "living well." This would include such things as performing virtuous acts, and enjoying one's social status. Virtues are acquired through practice; they become habitual. Good actions become an intrinsic part of a person's character.

Aristotle's outlook is a combination of absolutism and relativism. Some things, for Aristotle, are intrinsically wrong — absolutely — but he thought also that most feelings and actions are motivated by individual and relativistic reason. Unhappiness would come from attempting to make absolutes out of debatable propositions — those that are not rationally determined. Self-realization and development of character where good actions would be second nature: This was the main desire of Aristotle. Such a person would inherit happiness even without seeking it. A worthy model for a journalist's life could be taken from Aristotle: think, be moderate and develop a good character.

Immanuel Kant had a similar outlook but, unlike Aristotle's, his rationality was rational *a priori*. His moral person would be one who followed a predetermined maxim or principle that would assure the person's intrinsic worth. But it is not trying to be happy, said Kant, but living the kind of life whereby a person deserves to be happy. The virtuous person, for Kant, was the duty-bound person who followed principle without trying to predict consequences. Trust and obey: there's no other way. A kind of Christian perspective.

Then there was the utilitarian, John Stuart Mill, who exemplified those who would act so as to spread happiness as broadly as possible. Happy consequences; good consequences. Mill was more of an altruist than was Aristotle or Kant. These two were more interested in self-development and personal virtue than was Mill, who wanted to maximize happiness in the world.

There are journalists among us who gravitate largely toward inner development as did Aristotle and Kant and those who are more socially concerned like Mill. These are basic inclinations, often inconsistent and unclear but forming a thesis and antithesis, nevertheless. It would seem that Hegel's synthesis is what is needed for these journalists. Care for their own character and constant self-improvement, while at the same time evidencing deep concern for the improvement and happiness of others. This is the synthesis that the journalist — at least one with a humanistic orientation — must seek. It will solve many of the journalist's ideological problems, unravel many semantic quandaries and make for a well-balanced lifestyle. The journalist must seek a synthesis, or at least aspire to Aristotle's Golden Mean.

Finally, let us look briefly at Aristotle's mentor, Plato, whose thought, as we noted earlier, helped form the Great Thesis of Authoritarianism, against which the European Enlightenment libertarianism finally clashed. This early proponent of a highly structured society with philosopher kings in charge (with little of no salary) and the rest of the public fulfilling their special tasks might be compared to the elitist editor or news director who believes in a vertical hierarchy and would have little faith in communitarianism, although it may be developing into a viable synthesis. Today's media world still appears to be largely Platonic.

Plato wanted power in the hands of the best people possible, his philosopher kings. For him freedom (except for the rulers) was socially dysfunctional and would bring only conflict and contention. But he was realistic enough to know that not all people can be philosopher-kings. For him society must be vertically stratified. As Karl Popper has written, Plato cared little for democracy and favored stability and security over equality and freedom. Even propaganda (his "noble lies"), appealing to the emotions, was not a bad thing if it would help make society disciplined, smooth-running and law-abiding. Popper notes further that Plato insisted that "every trace of anarchy should be utterly eradicated from the life of all the men." The smooth-running institution or state insists that the person "keep one's place" and not stand out — for the individual, in Plato's mind, is "the Evil One himself." (Thorson, 1963, p. 59). This is similar to, but even stronger than, the old Chinese sage advice of social modesty and discipline.

The libertarians of the Age of Reason provided an antithesis to Plato's thought. They enthroned freedom, a scientific attitude, and egalitarianism. Plato's position, however, had been long in developing and was very powerful. So the synthesis that has grown out of the clash has left his authoritarian Thesis in a dominant position. Libertarians have revamped the Thesis, albeit slowly, through more democratization and public participation. A rather new synthesis — communitarianism — combining Platonic elitism and planned social structure with a heavy dose of democracy and community consciousness and power has emerged. It will be interesting to see how long this synthesis will last before itself being challenged by a rising antithesis.

CHAPTER 8

MISSION IMPOSSIBLE?

It is little wonder that, with all the conceptual uncertainties facing mass communication, plus all the unresolved dialectics seeking syntheses, some of them just mentioned, that the purpose or mission of the media remains a foundational question. In the United States, there seems a need for a mission, especially since the Constitution places the press above or beyond the law. The media establishment is the only institution to enjoy such power and prestige legally. Therefore, it is natural that one might wonder: Does the press have a core mission? In order to have such freedom, what obligations if any do the media owe society? Constitutionally, it has no mission, but this basic question has constantly haunted media scholars and workers. Does it not have a grand overarching reason for being? This is, in a very real sense, the pivotal question in mass communication.

Freedom poses the central problem. If the media are really free, they are free of any certain purpose or mission. So, in a way, freedom obviates any serious discussion of media mission. At least this is one position. Of course, even those libertarians who advance this position recognize that freedom *per se* is not a reasonable mission for the media. Free for what? This becomes the question and the "mission" takes priority. Ultimately libertarians are forced to fall back on a mission rationale of self-interest, of competition and profit-making. This is not exactly fair, however, for most libertarians claim a pluralism of missions, with their hierarchy of importance determined by various media managers. It is much simpler in authoritarian countries where a central person, group, or party determines the mission of the media — to support and publicize the social efforts of the authority.

In a country that permits substantial press freedom, the situation is quite different. There is uncertainty about mission. Or, said another way, there is a pluralism of missions, often overlapping but significantly varied. Freedom has splintered media unity of mission into fragmented emphases. In theory, constituencies in society are served (although not well: Hutchins Commission) by the media and that appears to be adequate as an overall mission. Brent Cunningham in *Columbia Journalism Review* (Nov./Dec. 2005.) remarks (p. 25) that a new mission might be developing with "public-service and idea-based journalism that helps set the agenda for what the nation thinks about." That's a big trinity of purpose. Accomplishing those three objectives would, indeed, usher in a new kind of journalism. But many journalists today would say that they are already doing this: providing a public service, presenting ideas, and setting a public agenda for discussion and concern.

There is no doubt but that the press has a mission. No doubt it is extremely important to different people in different ways. Fareed Zakaria, an insightful journalist and political analyst, says (2003, p. 231) that the press is really the only mediator in American society, explaining the world "to its public and its public to the world." That would be quite a mission in itself. But this job is not being done very well. Zakaria also notes that the media define reality and provide the political agenda. This, of course, is a very important part of a mission. Yet, says Zakaria, the press often inflames public passions, dramatizes, and trivializes news. Even so, the media are what we have and they obviously provide some desired product for various groups in society.

I

Even if it were true that media serve their several constituencies, would this be an adequate mission for the overall media system? Those who would say "yes" need to explain what is meant by "serve"

— something the Hutchins Commission (1947) did not do very well. The Commission, biased as it was by class, gender, education, and political philosophy, did make an attempt to establish some kind of mission for the press. Its conclusions, based on superficial "research," were mainly expressed negatively, stressing what the media were not doing that they should be doing. Ostensibly reporting on the state of freedom of the press in the United States, the Hutchins group focused on what they saw as weaknesses of the press, indicted the press as socially irresponsible and proceeded to propose what the press should do to be responsible.

It was with the Commission that the press theory of "social responsibility" made its way into the literature (Siebert, Peterson and Schramm, 1956). Naturally it was difficult for anyone to take issue with a theory wrapped in such glittering concepts as "public good" and "people's freedom." However, there were many (and they were in the press) who did, seeing the Commission as endangering the tenets of libertarianism. The academic community, however, was generally elated by the strong anti-individualist and social emphasis of the report (Commission on Freedom of the Press, 1947).

Prior to Hutchins it had been felt generally that the multiplicity of interpretations and news was what actually constituted not only a free press but also a responsible press. At least in the Western world, a "free press" in a democratic sense was seen as responsible *per se* to its social system. But no specific "mission statement" had existed for the press as a whole. Now there was one, created by the Hutchins Commission.

Seeing a clear danger in the growing restriction of media outlets and noting the general irresponsibility in American journalism (the criteria for responsibility, of course, set up by the Commission itself), the Hutchins group offered the ominous warning that "if they [the agencies of mass communication] are irresponsible, not even the First Amendment will protect their freedom from governmental control." It warned that if the press does not assume its responsibility, some other agency will see that the functions of mass communication are carried out. Coming from a notable group of intellectuals and getting wide publicity, such statements enraged most of the nation's editors and publishers at the time.

Well into the second half of the 20th century, the Commission's report received considerable attention. Then the issue largely settled down, journalists perhaps thinking that ignoring it was the best policy. But the report's ideas had taken root in the intellectual soil of the mass media and, together with growing stress on egalitarianism and public rights, still served as a catalyst for debate.

As to the media's mission, the Hutchins group made some sweeping (and in general some rather naïve) recommendations. For one, the press should provide full and truthful access to the day's "intelligence." Another: The press should give a representative picture of the constituent groups in the society. There were other recommendations, but these indicate the unrealistic idealism of the Commission. Or maybe it showed the commissioners' considerable ignorance of the way the press works.

At any rate, the 1947 report of the Hutchins Commission was an attempt to provide a purpose or mission for the press. But it failed within the libertarian parameters in which it was born. First Amendment freedom was questioned obliquely by the Commissioners, showing their inherent authoritarianism and opposition to a free market. Another criticism of the Commission was that its mission statement was so semantically unclear that it was, in essence, no mission at all.

What did the Commission mean when it said that the press should provide a "full" account of the day's news? Any account will, of course, never be full. Just how full did the Commission think it should be? No answer. Also: How would "truthfulness" in the press be measured? Would all statements quoted by the press have to be truthful? No answer. How would the press give a "representative picture of the constituent groups in the society"? The press cannot even isolate and name the constituent groups, much less give a "representative picture" of them.

Not everybody is really concerned about mission. Nihilists have an answer to the question of media mission: There is none. To speculate about it is meaningless. Media really have no significance in the total picture; journalism is an assortment of activities going off in all directions and accomplishing nothing. There is no purpose to journalism, or to anything else really. If you want to keep busy, all right. Work, but don't expect it to have any real significance or meaning. You could just as well be doing nothing, surviving from day to day, or perhaps being a street person. And if you disappear, so be it; your life will mean no more and no less than the most powerful people in the world. *Carpe diem* (get with it, enjoy) — or do nothing. It's all the same, for the world and life itself is really meaningless. Get out the paper but don't expect it to accomplish anything of significance. Forget this talk about mission.

The above is basically the philosophy of the media nihilist, and there are some of them here and there. Maybe not many, thankfully, but some. And they plant their hopeless and negative ideas among hopeful, idealistic journalists to the detriment of media mission and morality. Of course there is no meaning to journalism, to media mission — or to life itself — unless we give it meaning. So, basically, the nihilistic journalist is one whose meaningless existence cannot propose any mission to the media. But if a journalist has a personal mission within the media — a purpose for being in the media — then this purpose will project itself to the media institution itself in the form of a mission.

II

So perhaps we have the beginning at least of a discussion about mission. Mission depends on the purposes we assign to the media, no more and no less. In the vastness of the American press we have every kind of medium imaginable. It is true that giant conglomerates are owning growing segments of the media, but within these empires there are all kinds of media. We have already discussed three main types of media: (1) the class media, (2) the mass media and (3) the crass media. Each of these types has a mission — respectively, to stimulate intellectually, to inform practically; to gratify emotionally, to practically inform; and to emotionally gratify.

What does this have to do with media mission? Perhaps very little beyond reflecting a general capitalistic proclivity to appeal to educational/attitudinal members of the market. Class, race, gender, educational level, IQ, public consciousness and other factors enter into this mix of media emphases. It is a complex communications network that favors some, neglects others and ignores others. This much is certain: The media network is not an equal opportunity provider.

Perhaps the mission of "the press" is to be missionless. Or, said another way, maybe it should be multi-mission in nature. Let's take one newspaper, for example. *The Washington Post* is reputed to be "liberal," and let us assume that it is. If so, what is its mission or purpose? To be "fair and balanced" sounds good, but I doubt if it a realistic mission of many journalists. Why should a liberal newspaper be balanced? If the newspaper published 50% of its articles with a liberal slant and the other 50% with a conservative slant, would that be balanced coverage. Maybe, in a way. But it would not be in sync with the *Post*'s mission.

Okay. The *Post* is liberal. It is part of its mission. Another newspaper, *The Indianapolis News*, for instance, is conservative. And other papers across the country have their missions on a liberal-conservative spectrum. Some seem to have no mission at all so far as political or ideological bias is concerned. So we could say that "the press" (the totality) has no mission or it has a pluralistic mission. This aspect of mission, of course, is related only to political purpose. Newspapers have other purposes or commitments — some mainly to general news, some to featurized entertainment, some to business, some to sports and some to local news. Therefore, asking about the "mission" of "the press" becomes meaningless rhetoric if one is looking for a single answer.

Some say that the press's mission is to let the people know. The "right to know" myth has already been discussed, so we will not belabor that. But it is interesting to note that circulation figures and serious programs in the electronic media show that most people do not really want to know. When and if they do, they will still not know all they perhaps need to know but will know more than they presently do. So the responsibility for the acquisition of information falls on the audience as well as on the media. Recognition of this fact goes a long way to lessen the importance often given to the responsibility of the media to inform. Some might say that it obviates a mission of news provision.

Beyond providing information, then, what could be the purpose of the media? The only other thing really is to entertain. What else do people need (or even want) from public communication? So this would mean that we can say with some certainty that the mission of the media is to inform and to entertain. So we have solved the problem. We have come up with the media's mission: To inform and entertain.

We are talking, of course, about the United States. In other countries the media could certainly add one other plank (and it would be the main one) to its mission statement: to support the government or some special social group. They would also inform and entertain to some degree. So they would have a trinary mission instead of a dual mission as in a libertarian, market-based society.

That media in some countries have the primary mission of supporting the government should not be overlooked by American observers. Plato established the mission indirectly for the media by stressing political and collective utilitarianism (Popper) in his political philosophy. Following Plato, the media would do only what was in the interest of the state. What was just, what was good, would be only what was for the unity and stability of the society as determined by the leadership of the state. The press's mission, then, would be to serve the collective whole, not the interests of multiple managers of the media.

III

So have we solved the mission question? In general terms, maybe. But still, as we seek an overall mission concept, we are not satisfied. There seems to be no general theory. We can say that information and entertainment (and social direction) form the universal purpose of the public media but is that enough? Such purposes are more tactical than strategic and they say little about a mission beyond simply providing information and entertainment. It would be like saying that the mission of a school is to provide education. Education for what purpose?

Information for what purpose? Entertainment for what purpose? The obvious answer: So that people can know more and be happier. Why, we might ask, should people know more? And could not they be as happy without the public media? At one time in history people entertained themselves and found out the information they needed without public communication. Did they become happy (or happier) with the advent of public communication? No answer. Pushing the question of mission back and back, we find that describing it may well be impossible. And perhaps unnecessary, except for very mundane and practical reasons.

We have seen that the media are diversified, and this pluralism appears to be a good enough mission on its own — to provide a broad range of information and entertainment to choose from. But wait! What about the "quality" of the information. Is giving people many and varied messages a good thing if these messages are poor to middling? Providing good information is more important than providing much information. Of course, if the media can enlighten the people with information quantity and quality, that would be the ideal — and a worthy mission. What happens, of course, is that information — sound and unsound, helpful and harmful — from diverse sources flows among the audiences constantly, is selected almost randomly by the audience members and helps structure individual perceptions of the world.

In view of what has been said, it might be enough to propose that the overriding mission of the public media is to provide a platform for a great number of missions that flow from class, mass and crass media to their respective audiences. If the media did not provide agenda to guide the thinking and talking of people, human conversations would indeed be narrow and parochial. So, perhaps we can say that the media arrange and rearrange the furniture of our world, trying albeit unsuccessfully to reflect the dynamism of the reality around us.

A big concern in the United States today is democratization — of the society and of the media. The communitarians are at the forefront of this concern. It is certainly, for them at least, an important part of the media's mission. Listen to what the German scholar Michael Kunczik says about this (266): "Participation of the people is most important, since the more widespread a person's participation in collective decision-making and the greater their integration into the communication structure, the higher is the commitment to the nation state ... ." Kunczik adds a second task for the media: to prevent the establishment of oligarchic leadership. A worthy task, no doubt. But oligarchies are everywhere, so obviously media are failing in ridding societies of them. Oligarchic leadership, Kunczik says, is fundamentally harmful to democracy, for it results in apathy and alienation of the governed. What about the oligarchy of the media establishment itself? Kunczik does not get into that, but it may well account for much apathy and alienation in journalism.

As for citizen participation in media decision-making, there has been almost none. True, public (civic) journalism has made a small impact, but it has not caught on in the American press. And as for the prevention of oligarchy, the media have done nothing. Since the media themselves are governed by the powerful few, it is not strange that they would not oppose the same situation in government. Around the world, outside Europe and America, this democratic mission for the press is hardly ever mentioned. So it is safe to say that it is simply an ideal in the minds of certain ideological segments in the Western World. But it does form part of the multi-faceted mission.

It seems that in the United States we must try to spread our ideas among the nations. What we have in journalism are missionaries without a mission — or at least a well-defined one. American intellectuals — including some journalists — who breeze through the world visiting media and press groups, tend to propagate the faith of U.S.-style journalism. Instead of helping them develop a consistent press theory and practice of their own, American media spokesmen, at every opportunity try to indoctrinate foreign cultures with their own values. But their values are incomplete, hazy and often counter-productive to the cultures they are trying to reform. It took me a while to realize this, but quite early I abdicated my missionary zeal. The true libertarian in the media should first try to develop a meaningful mission at home, then be content to have other countries work out their own media salvation.

Three main factors basically form a media system's mission: (1)

diversity of individual purposes, (2) unified policy of the national leadership and (3) a single goal by voluntary media consensus. The first is a vague and normless one, a kind of mission that is no mission; the second is a centrally directed mission; and the third is a kind of media cooperative determination of purpose.

This having been said, the mission of the media is still problematic. Perhaps, like having a media code of ethics, a mission is a many-splintered thing evolving and devolving with each passing year and generation. Although it is difficult for American journalists (or anyone else) to talk about the media's mission, they keep on trying. For instance an editorial in *Columbia Journalism Review* (March/April 2005) expresses an encapsulated version with this head: "On Mission: It's Time to Reconnect the Press and the Public." Reconnecting press and public is easy to say but difficult to realize. And the editorialist did not say how this was to be done except that it was the press's job to "watchdog (sic) our government." Maybe, in some cases, that is the press's job. But for many media systems it might as well be to "support our government." And, even in the United States, it is hardly the mission of a free press to be a watchdog.

The mission of bringing about an egalitarian society, of promoting equality, is often set up as a major one for the media. Harvard philosopher John Rawls is a great proponent of equality as a handmaiden of democracy. This, it would seem, is proposing that both media and governments surrender their special elite positions to a society of equals. Rawls' Theory of Justice (1971) attempts to equate equality with fairness, which does not seem rational to me. And seeing equality as a handmaiden of democracy is even more problematic. The citizens who vote in leaders are no longer equal to those leaders. Inequality in public life and in the media appears much more reasonable and in keeping with meritocracy and natural law.

Social impact: This is an oft-stated goal or mission of the press. Standing alone, however, it is extremely vague, especially in its moral dimensions. Cliff Christians (Land, p. 65), coming from a communitarianism perspective, goes so far as to advocate that the press mission should be reformed from neutrality to civic transformation. "A revitalized citizenship becomes the aim of the press

— not merely readers and audiences provided with information, but morally literate persons." Journalists with whom I have talked about this are stunned by Christians' assertion and think that their desire to provide information in an objective and unbiased news is the primary mission. They would leave civic transformation up to the politicians and social workers. This may be, but as University of Missouri professor Lee Wilkins has observed (Land, p. 23), communitarians like Christians have predicted that their philosophy will be the "next appropriate base for journalism." It well may be as the world struggles increasingly against social insecurity, postmodernist relativism and irresponsible public communication.

Another view of mission came from France. Alexis de Tocqueville, in his mid-19th century visit to America, predicted the helpful inroads that communitarianism would make but offered some warnings. In the second volume of *Democracy in America*, he got into a discussion of public societies or associations and saw newspapers as essential to the enhancement of a community, saying that without them there would no common activity. But he warned of the possibility that in the future citizens might well be assimilated and lost in the anonymity of the community. He would urge the media to fight against this tendency, while at the same time enhance a sense of helpful association. They were needed also, he wrote, to protect freedom and maintain civilization. Although he prized freedom (vol. 1), he felt, like the Hutchins Commission later on, that American newspapers used their freedom irresponsibly by invading privacy and stressing the negative and the sensational.

Mission — whatever it is exactly — has some relationship to media morality, to underlying principle and to the right and wrong actions of the media. A mission can be moral or immoral — and sometimes it is some of both. Perhaps it is well that we cannot specify a mission for the media. Clarity of overall mission may simply indicate an authoritarian media system, one that would regiment the media and make a discussion of ethics unnecessary. In fact with a clear and universally accepted mission, one wonders if there could really be a media morality. At any rate, let us take a brief look at this complex subject of morality.

CHAPTER 9

MORALITY

So much has been written and spoken about ethics in the mass media that it is difficult to know where to start a conversation on the subject. The great emphasis given it today attests to its importance, or perceived importance, by media practitioners, communication educators and the general public. Every fall from ethical practice, especially by media leaders like *The Washington Post, The New York Times* and CBS News darkens the cloud that hangs over journalism and the media generally.

Morality is a multi-sided thing — a state of character that derives from rationalism and mysticism, from personal and social concern, and from habitual, virtuous acts based on a concern for consequences and/or pre-determined principle. It is part rational and part emotional. It is part deterministic and part instinctive. It is part egoistic and part social. It is part secular and part religious. The communicator is caught often on the proverbial horns of a dilemma. While being faithful to one ethical theory, he or she is minimizing or evading another. To some instinct is enough; for others ethics is a rational concern.

Being ethical, then, is theoretically relative. Good philosophical representatives of this dilemma are Immanuel Kant and John Stuart Mill. With his concern for consequences, Mill could pronounce a certain action ethical while Kant, with his predetermined legalism, would not. Other theories whirl about us: social contract, virtue, instinctual and divine command (to name a few). It's a wild ethical world out there.

And then there are those communicators, Machiavellians at heart, who enthrone pragmatism and care little for humanistic ethics. They have a selfish motivation. Something that works is better than something that doesn't. Results dominate over principle. Other Machiavellians of a different kind are among mass communicators: They may be called Kautilyans, wanting to use any means necessary to achieve an altruistic end. In India, at least five centuries before Machiavelli, a political adviser named Kautilya (Merrill, 2005) mixed pragmatism with a compassion for the poor, for women and slaves. He proposed harsh, sometimes ruthless, technologies to get things done, but his actions had an overlay of morality. So, although he was a forerunner of Machiavelli, his motivation, unlike Machiavelli's, was to aid social welfare and not to protect the sovereign.

One might say that the American pragmatic philosopher John Dewey was a kind of modern Kautilyan without the harsh edges, dedicated to moral flexibility without strict rule-based commitment. This view has been criticized (Richards, p. 140) for not having enough respect for shared values and rules, but Dewey's pragmatic ethical reasoning has many supporters who value its creativity and inventiveness. As with Kautilya, Dewey would stress the collective good. He would see individual journalists as submerging their personal desires so as to benefit the group or community. He (Dewey, 1963, pp. 65-67), like the communitarians of today, saw the Enlightenment as wrong in its emphasis on the individual, when collective progress is what is important. He did not really ignore the individual but redefined it as a "new" kind that puts the person in a social context that makes it harmonious with social action.

Today we have the public-service Kautilyans and the egocentric Machiavellians. It seems that all journalists are to some degree Machiavellian of one or both types, thriving on the scoop and the big story regardless of how they manage to get it — to give them personal or institutional prestige or to serve some segment of the public. Perhaps there is a basic success-orientation built into the very fiber of a journalist — a great competitive spirit that is able to justify almost any means to achieve what they consider a "higher" telos.

As Karl Popper points out, Plato's criterion for morality, not quite so pointedly negative as Machiavelli's, was the interest of the state. The media, therefore, should serve to help with the "political hygiene" by supporting and cooperating with the state leadership. Here, in the morality of some nations, is (in Plato's view) the media's mission: What facilitates or furthers the interest of the state is good and virtuous, and what weakens or threatens it is bad, wicked and unjust.

At the base of most communication ethics, in the Western World at least, is the concept of truth. But for many, truth can be dangerous, and not only that, it can be "unethical" in some cases. But it persists as a foundation stone of ethics. That the public has a right to expect the truth is a journalistic truism, even if is ignored often in practice. Some communicators even question this basic and ask: Who says that a journalist, for example, must be truthful? Where does such a rule come from? In spite of Kant's impressive Categorical Imperative, there are those (and they are not all irrational) who would not want truthfulness universalized.

Half-truths, distortions, and outright censorship dominate in the media world. And this is not surprising, say the postmodernists who believe that actually there is no truth — or any truth is as good as any other truth. If this is the case, then how can we take this postmodern concept as a truthful one? In a way, these postmodernists are fatalists, accepting the impossibility of truthful reporting and resigning themselves to a multi-framed reality in journalism. What we need is not fatalism but the acceptance of what Australian communication scholar Ian Richards (22) has called "criteria of rational acceptability." Such criteria, it is said (Richards, 27-31), include accuracy, completeness, fairness and objectivity. In short, truth in journalism is what can be reasonably expected — not some metaphysical Platonic form of truth. Attitude and intention enter into this rational acceptability; for example, a basic desire by the reporter to be as truthful as possible, to have a motivation to accuracy and completeness. I am not so sure about fairness and objectivity. In my view "fairness" is one of the most semantically problematic of all concepts, and "objectivity" connotes an overarching fullness and perfection that is not rationally possible.

So it can be said that audiences see through a glass darkly; they see only the shadows of reality, and usually they are the sensational and negative shadows. The "truth" in communication is the truth that is created by encoders, refined by communicators and formed by audiences (decoders). Behind this communicated truth may be the "real" world, but our communicators and audiences will never see it.

And it may be a good thing that they don't. It would be too much for the person to bear — seeing the real world in all its detail would send humanity into a psychotic tailspin. Communicators and mass media are needed to act as fallout shelters for the people, to filter reality for peace of mind, to provide information that can be handled by the people.

Most Western philosophers, outside religion, have posited that truth and reason are inseparably connected. Thus, the irrational person can never find the truth. Many sages of religion (hakim and other priests and aesthetes) would disagree with this view. Suhrawardi, for example (Walbridge), among the most outstanding of the Islamic philosophers (12th century), maintained that mystical intuition was the only tool for discovering the truth. He has had many supporters in this contention, especially in Buddhism and Taoism. Suhrawardi, an "illuminationist" and a sufi, combined the mysticism of his native Persia with the primary philosophy of the time — Platonism. There are also Western philosophers who maintain that truth transcends our thought processes and that moral judgments are not rational, as David Hume believed, and that they are only individual attitudes or preferences. A person is "illuminated" or infused with moral assurance, not by thought-processes but by a kind of transcendent or metaphysical inner voice. But this view is more oriental than occidental. Western journalists may often seem to be in a kind of trance, but it is not the trance of transcendental meditation.

Simplifying reality: Is this the real importance of the media? If they are able to help in the progress and discipline of society they must be "agenda-setters" (simplifiers), as Max McCombs and others have said. But simplifying may lead to oversimplifying, causing people to live in a childish, unrealistic world. And one problem with mass communication setting people's agenda — or things to consider important — is that much of what the media disseminate is trivial, mind-numbing, vulgar, or inaccurate. And the moral question of agenda-setting comes up: What ought to be the agenda that the media set? Of course, if the media had leaders like Plato's philosopher-kings, the conservative and socially harmonizing agenda-setting would likely lead to a more congenial, safer, and duller society and public conversation.

I

Perhaps a good place to launch a discussion of media ethics is to consider again the purpose of the media. This, of course, varies from medium to medium, from society to society. But we can assume that media want to inform, entertain and interpret. The entertaining purpose offers the greatest ethical danger. But information, too, is problematic due to the nature of the information and its gathering. As for interpretation, a medium may well persuade, steer their audiences in certain directions, not all of them helpful. The ethical assumption is that media will be honest, fair, balanced and truthful in their efforts — but we know that such an assumption is unrealistic.

The pragmatic assumption, a more realistic one, is that the media will serve their owners and interests, provide a propaganda outlet for some special elite, or do what is necessary to survive, or serve the public interest. It is possible that the media can do all four, but it is doubtful. If we talk about the media in Saudi Arabia, we have different expectations than if we are talking about the British media. Media ideology stemming from political realities of a society affects ethical perspectives and, to a large degree, determines media freedom and purpose.

Media in a free press system are not bound by statist or social control ethical considerations and may resort to propaganda, falsification, agitation, distortion, bias and communication that may be socially harmful. However, Walter Lippmann and others have pointed out that press freedom rests on the assumption that the media will provide serious material that will permit the citizens to be wise and well-informed voters. It is not the freedom to do anything. The person concerned with media morality would tend to agree with Lippmann, but the problem is the determination of what is socially and politically helpful and what is not. Unfortunately our media managers are not Plato's philosophers, although they may have his penchant for direct leadership.

Certainly the wide entertainment activities of the media would not make for more enlightened voters or help society to progress. Actually media reality is perhaps just the opposite: to narcotize the citizenry into passivity and curb their critical inclinations. At any rate humanity manages to muddle along and the media, by and large, satisfy a basic need, however poorly, and, as businesses or government bulletin boards, do very well.

In any nation with a non-governmental press, the purposes of the media are varied. A monolithic concept will exist only in an authoritarian country. For a media system that contends to have little or no government interference, we must say there is no underlying purpose or objective. There are many purposes and they often conflict with one another. Inform the public; entertain the public; make money. And many others.

After looking at ethical codes around the world (Cooper, et al., 1985), it is fair to say that the most common ethical imperative seems to be truth-telling. Truth, of course, means many things to different media. The metaphysical truth cannot be told, so the media need not worry about that. The kind of truth they are concerned with comprise bits and pieces of the truth they select from the wide-world of truth, the selected and communicated truth. Not the whole truth, of course; that is impossible. So, what this means is that the media's version of the truth is their truth. And since various media provide differing versions of "the truth," the people never really know exactly what to believe. Journalism is a matter of faith. People believe something of the hodge-podge of material they access from the media and from a few private conversations. One's synthesis of the varieties of media-produced information is about the only truth he or she will get. Unless, of course, the person has some kind of instinctive or spiritual connection to the supernatural.

II

If you are a Platonic idealist, behind the manifest or phenomenal world of ethics exists a perfect world of morality. The perfect moral world. Portions of this world break out occasionally into our everyday lives in the form of good intentions, wise decisions and helpful actions. But ethics, like truth, is always shrouded in the mists of human values, biases and expediencies. The most conscientious communicator, with a Kantian will to be ethical, is never sure of his or her success. One of the uncertainties of life is ethical action, whether a person follows a pre-determined maxim or considers the consequences of an action. Or, I should add, whether one "senses" or "intuits" what should be done.

Let us consider briefly the first two of these uncertainties. Often they are called "theories of ethics" — the legalistic (deontological) and the utilitarian (teleological). These are exemplified , alternatively by the great philosophers Immanuel Kant and John Stuart Mill.

What a mass communicator should do, Kant would say, is to be duty-bound to follow a rationally formed maxim or principle. Follow it and you will act ethically. Fail to follow it and you will act unethically. Don't worry about consequences, Kant would say. What one needs to do is to be faithful to principle. Such an ethics is too cold and formalistic for many; it does not allow rational flexibility. Another problem is that we can never be sure that the principle we follow is an ethical one. Kant would answer: Whatever you would be willing that all people do is the standard of ethics. Also he would insist that all people be treated as ends, never as means. And he would put great stress on "intentions," on motives for an action, on the will to act correctly.

Mill, on the other hand, would base one's actions on consideration of consequences. He would, as a utilitarian, want to bring the greatest happiness (pleasure, good) to the greatest number. And he would, unlike Kant, be willing to adjust ethical action to the particular situation. He would have people act for a purpose, not out of an obligation to follow a rule. A problem, of course, with such an ethical theory is that one can rationalize almost any action by foreseeing all kinds of consequences. The journalist, for example, can justify stealing papers from an official's desk by believing that the public knowledge of the papers will result in the people's greatest happiness. Many shady actions have occurred in journalism by the rationale that the people have a right to know. How would a journalist, for example, evaluate the nature of actions as to their ethics?

Three ways are usually suggested (Porter): (1) Intentionalism — the motive of the agent, (2) Teleologism — the importance of the outcomes, and (3) Formalism — the nature of the act itself. We have discussed these earlier in other terms, but this triad shows the often contradictory evaluative criteria used in moral philosophy and points up the problems many people have with varying ethical verdicts. The sociologist Max Weber, in the mid-20th century, proposed two kinds of ethics (Kunczik): (a) the ethic of responsibility and (b) the ethic of conviction. An editor, for example, would judge the correctness of a story according to its foreseeable consequences, or from the conviction motivating the action. Weber, however, does not see these two guiding principles as absolute opposites, and they can work together in what I have called (1989) the "deontelec" ethical synthesis.

People are confused about ethics. As well they might be. Values vary. Traditions dictate different actions. Wise leaders contradict each other. Religions clash. Ideologies fashion moralities, and politicians often take the expediency road. Even in a more formal, academic sense, ethics is tied to theories. If a communicator, for instance, acts on the basis of a Kantian (or deontological) theory, he or she is ethical. If another acts on a Millian (or teleological or consequence) theory, he or she is ethical The fact that they might be acting in opposing ways seems to make no difference. They are ethically motivated. And if another person acts purely out of instinct or immediate "feeling," then that person is also ethical — if the action is motivated by good will.

Many communicators have trouble with this. One action must be more ethical than another, regardless of the actor's motivation, they say. Philosophers from the days of Confucius and Socrates have wrestled with this objection. There seems to be no firm answer. No definite ethical answer can be given for every moral quandary. Cases can be discussed, positions can be argued, but no firm answers can be given. Probably the closest anyone can come is to stress one of Kant's basics: The only thing that is good without question is a good will It seems to me that if one combines this Kantian ethics with Aristotle's virtue-ethics, this combination will provide the highest morality. Being virtuous (having courage, moderation, liberality, magnanimity and the rest of Aristotle's list) plus having a good will for their use and strong sense of duty to them (Kant) should assure moral superiority. Virtue is acquired by habitually performing humane and altruistic acts without neglecting self-enhancing habits that assure a solid character.

Good will is built into good character. A good character is one that predominantly acts according to the highest standards of the community and has an attitude of desiring to do what is right. Being virtuous. Having self-respect. To accomplish this, communicators must be concerned with living up to their potential, doing the right thing, and developing themselves beyond the materialistic aspects of their lives. One must develop good habits, as Aristotle and Confucius emphasized, and should not act out of expediency or emotion.

Indian leader Mohandas Gandhi said that good habits are the key to an ethical life. Before trying to reform society, said Gandhi, one must reform one's self.

Of course, concepts like self-respect are troublesome. For instance, the ancient Athenean character, epitomized largely in Homer's epic tales, was this: striving for excellence and trying to go beyond all others. This self-transcendent emphasis was similar to that propounded much later by Nietzsche. It is this self-oriented philosophy that, for some, is what leads to self-respect.

One ethics scholar has written that journalists who falsify, embellish and plagiarize their stories are guided by a philosophic framework called "ethical egoism." I must disagree with this assertion. Such a journalist is guided by nothing that can be called "ethical." An ethical egoist is one who strives to be ethical according to his or her own drive to do the right thing. The falsifying and plagiarizing journalist is not trying to be ethical. We should call the unethical journalist by the proper label — unethical. Or maybe "ethical nihilist." I would say that all journalists who try to do the right thing are ethical "egoists," even if they take their cues from moral exemplars.

But there is the self-effacing, more humble, more altruistic ethical stance, fostered largely by Mo Tzu and other Oriental thinkers and religious savants (Kupperman), where self-respect comes from turning attention away from self to others. This socially conscious orientation probably began early — in the West with the pro-Socratic Greek philosopher Pythagoras (about 500 B.C.), who even saw private property as the root of all evil and who may have been the first communist.

Any serious discussion of ethics must note its dual nature. Emphasis on self and self-improvement is, of course, important. But so also is a concern for others and for society. We have a dualism of emphasis: individualism and socialism. C. S. Lewis, noted British author, has pointed out the need for concern for both individual and social ethics. We must, he said, "tidy up" our inner lives before playing the part of social engineers. Ethicists of this persuasion are descendents of Enlightenment thinkers like Locke, Voltaire, Jefferson and Madison.

Another notable individualist ethical thinker was David Hume (1711-1776). Like Aristotle, his emphasis was on character-building, on personal dedication to habitual allegiance to virtue. Objective: the "moral" person, the basically good person who, however may well do unethical acts now and then. Human interaction was important to Hume (after all, he was a utilitarian), but his main concern was personal moral development. Unlike many communitarians of today, Hume saw egoist ethics as personal moral development that reinforced the group; in fact, he echoed Aristotle and Confucius as believing that a good person will actively seek a good society or community.

The theologian Reinhold Niebuhr, although a strong proponent of media responsibility, saw the danger inherent in communitarianism to foster conformity, and this he saw as bad. Certainly no David Hume, but he saw the weakness of community-based values disseminated through the public media. Writing in 1957 (p. xix), Niebuhr noted that the community can become "a tyrant" by becoming the arbiter of opinion," that makes nonconformity difficult through the weight of standardized opinion. And Lewis Lapham, a modern journalist, echoes the voice of Hume and Niebuhr and warns communicators not to give up their individual ethical decision-making to some group.

Closely related to individualism, in fact perhaps an extreme form of it, is what I have called elsewhere (Merrill, 1996) existential journalism. Many critics have seen this as narcissistic or egocentric journalism and have regretted the day I came up with that term. They say it gives too much emphasis to freedom. At the same time they cry, "Give us answers. We must do something to improve the press, to give it credibility, to raise it up above mediocrity and depravity." They would enthrone social responsibility, not freedom.

The existentialist would also enthrone responsibility — but personal responsibility. I have maintained that an existentialist stance might be just the answer we need. Perhaps it is only the individual communicator, acting authentically and progressively, that can make some kind of impact. Now with the new media added to the old and personalized verbal interaction becoming important, freedom — the quiddity of existentialism — has become increasingly possible. I have proposed an acronymic formula for existential journalism — F-I-C-A-R (freedom-individualism-commitment-action-responsibility). The first letter (freedom) is essential, but the last one — responsibility — must control and curtail this freedom.

Contrary to common belief, existentialists, cousins of the Romanticists and Transcendentalists, require of themselves responsibility. In fact, the existential communicator places it, along with freedom, as an ideal. It is what saves him or her from orgiastic gushes of egoistic subjectivity. Accepting personal responsibility is a heavy burden and the existential communicator takes it seriously. Just where this sense of responsibility comes from is not clear, but it is there just as surely as if it had come from Kantian legalism or Millian utilitarianism. The existential communicator has it, perhaps intuiting it from some metaphysical source or inferring it from a sense of personal and social concern.

But, in today's world, social or communitarian ethical thinkers seem to be in the majority. They have a long history, starting back in the Fourth century B.C. with the Chinese philosopher Hsun Tzu who resembled Plato in his regimented, groupist ethics. Hsun's follower

Han Fei believed human nature to be rebellious and evil and, like the French philosopher Rousseau, thought that the community always has precedence over the individual. What was good and ethical was what was good for society. And Hegel concurred — the individual must sacrifice self to the society (state).

The contemporary Irish-born philosopher and novelist Iris Murdoch has reinforced this communitarian stance. A deep concern for connecting with others and a strong altruistic impulse highlights her moral philosophy. Taking a counter position to the American Ayn Rand, who was a proponent of rational self-interest, Murdoch urges that we reach "the good" by shedding egoist proclivities, by stressing rational interest in the community. A media person today, following Murdoch, would definitely have the communitarian desire for "civic transformation." She, like the eminent modern philosopher Hannah Arendt, Theologian Martin Buber and the historian Barbara Tuchman, would tell the journalist that he or she must connect with others to create a moral community.

This emphasis that is gaining popularity in public communication circles, at least in a modified way, has come to be called communitarianism. Its followers believe that the ethical person is one who sublimates personal ethical values to societal expectations and needs. It is an emphasis that provides a sound foundation for social ethics, but it has a seed of danger within it. A communicator's sense of self-esteem and self-reliance may be at risk. As Ayn Rand believes, following the spirit of Aristotle and Spinoza (both critics of self-sacrifice and altruism), the human life is the moral standard, and it should be a happy life that values self-enhancement and rationality. According to Rand, a real danger to the human person is the cult of communitarian promoters with their goal of egalitarianism, community cooperation and social stability.

III

Although the concept of ethics is highly problematic, there are some rather substantial things we can say about it. Ethical acts stem from a basic life-plan, a philosophy of life, a concern for seeking the good, a desire to do what we ought to do. Before any communicator chooses any particular ethics, he or she must decide whether or not to be ethical. This is the obvious beginning. There is a tendency today to identify as "ethical" almost anything. What I want to do, I do; therefore, it is ethical for me to do it. This, as philosophers say is the "naturalistic fallacy" — assuming that the "is" is the "ought." In layman's terms, it is extremely childish and washes away any real meaning to "ethics," making every action ethical.

It is true that ethics has to do with "self-legislation" and "self-enforcement," unlike law. We know when a person is doing an illegal act, but are often perplexed about the ethics of a person's actions. It is important to note that ethics deals with the voluntary actions, motivated by good will. If a communicator has no control over his or her actions, then there is no need to talk about ethics. Voluntary actions are those that a communicator could have done differently if desired. This is why in a real sense it is useless to criticize the ethics of a journalist who works in an authoritarian country. This journalist does not have the luxury of deciding among alternative actions. The existentialist might disagree with this by saying that a person always has the power of refusing to follow orders and that such refusal would be an ethical decision. In some ideal world this might be the case, but in this world of practicality it is too much to expect. Ethical decisions must be made within the context of reasonable expectations.

But how does a communicator know when a message is good or bad? Ethical or unethical? He or she can follow Kant and test it against his Categorical Imperative. Would the communicator be willing to see the message (and its method of acquisition) universalized? Or would the communicator agree with Bertrand Russell that the right conduct is what produces the greatest balance of satisfaction over dissatisfaction regardless of who enjoys it? Or would the communicator see the best action as that which enhances or her self-worth, self-respect, enduring character and sense of well-being? Or would the communicator simply resort to instinct and a kind of metaphysical intuition to give an answer to what is good or bad, better or worse? Or would the communicator step up the moral ladder (Dewey) simply by progressing, however small the steps? Or would the communicator call an action "ethical" if it were done from a good motive (Kant) — a will to do the right thing?

And then there are ethicists who simply say that there are no real standards for ethical behavior, that calling something ethical is simply saying that the person agrees with the action. Further complicating the matter is what is called the "indirect" view of ethics that focuses on the person and not on the act. A person may be an ethical person, although from time to time he or she may do unethical things. This position comes closest to the Aristotelian concept of being a principled or virtuous person, one who has developed a good "character."

Existentialist Karl Jaspers was talking about that type of principled person. His ideal journalist would be honest, well-informed, rational, authentic, sincere, active and willing to take personal responsibility for his or her actions. In short, this journalist would be virtuous, a person of good intentions, self-control and wisdom.

Commitment to principled action is very important for journalists (Lambeth, 1986), and virtue that endures is indeed praiseworthy. Strong will, for Nietzsche, was the way to transvalue normal life and rise to a moral level where constant ethical decision-making is unnecessary. But the journalist is prone to akrasia, where moral integrity can easily deteriorate into self-rewarding action. Maybe the best way to test one's moral stability is to wear Gyges' magical ring (Plato, *Republic*, Book II) that makes one invisible and raises the question: Would I stick to my principles if nobody could see me and my actions? It's a good one: the invisible man test.

IV

A concern with actions is the main focus of communication ethics. What is being done that is good or bad, right or wrong, better or worse?

Current problems in communication ethics largely deal with such things as fabrication, plagiarism, invasion of privacy, and the concealment of the names of sources. Journalists in big and small media have faced these problems, have been criticized, fired and even jailed. But such unethical practices go on. The four mentioned above are, of course, among the big ethical issues that face the modern communicator. Dozens of others fill the media world. Quoting out of context, imprecise paraphrasing, incorrect quotations, misidentifications, appealing to prurient interests, biased news and propaganda, conflicts of interest, sensationalism and negativism, and on and on.

What can be done about it? Probably little in our highly competitive, entertainment-based society where Machiavellian success and hedonistic motives hold sway. At least there seems little the government can do about it. But the media managers themselves could, if they would, bring about some improvement. They could, as noted 21st century reporter Bill Kovach has said, create an atmosphere where such questionable acts are not tolerated. Plenty of evidence exists that the degradation of the journalist is rampant in the world, due largely to the rebellious nature of man. We know the depths to which mass communicators can sink, but we also recognize the heights that have been achieved by media people. From the Age of Reason, we learned that journalists could achieve these heights on their own, unassisted. This belief has now been all but lost in the face of social massification, networking, and organized and cooperative accomplishments. The lone voice has been drowned out in the clamor of diverse groups and organizations.

What today's journalists, in the midst of their alienation, have forgotten is that even lost in the anonymity of the mass media, they still have an individual spirit and its power. They may not individually change institutions, but they can unquestionably change themselves. And to some extent, others. Spirit ultimately triumphs over material power. Spirit — the will to become better and greater — resides in every journalist. George Thomas in his *Spirit and Its Freedom*, has defined spirit as the creative activity helping people rationally to understand universal truth and serve others with a love derived from their divine potentialities. Spirit, indeed, is a kind of creative activity, and it is assumed that such activity will be progressive and helpful to society. This assumption, however, may be mistaken.

At least we can say that spirit is tangential to, but not separated from, a daily consideration of ethical concerns of the journalist. In some of these problematic ethical areas, such as use of anonymous sources, there is disagreement among media managers. Just how will the spirit move the journalist? Ben Bradlee, when editor of *The Washington Post*, at one time was moved by the spirit to ban unnamed sources from his newspaper. But the pressures were too great, the competitors were getting good stories that the *Post* was missing. So the bold experiment failed. It is obviously difficult for a media leader to stand by his or her ethical principles. Of course, Bradlee could have justified unnamed sources by appealing to the teleological theory, saying that the story (even without a named source) should be told and the people needed to know the information. At any rate, writes Ben Bagdikian (1997), unnamed sources serve too many purposes in our society and will not be disappearing in the near future.

Hiding sources' names may continue to have a bright future, but one thing must be considered by conscientious reporters. A story without a source, contends semanticist S. I. Hayakawa, is not a report. Why? Because the receiver of the report has no way to confirm whether what is said to have been said is really what was said. There is no source to go to. Therefore, so far as the audience is concerned, the story or the part attributed to an unnamed source, can be pure fiction.

V

Practical, everyday ethical problems and cases can (and are) discussed almost *ad nauseam*, and ethicists, professional and amateur, enthusiastically suggest their solutions. Seminars, conferences, institutes and academic courses have proliferated, propounding the intricacies of media ethics. Ethics "coaches" hold forth in some newsrooms. One would think that the ethical conduct of the media would be getting better. But one would be wrong. If anything, the situation is getting worse, not only in crass and mass media but also in the class media like *The Washington Post, The New York Times, The New Yorker*, and NPR. The public often hears of their shortcomings, while only the journalists at less prominent media know the questionable activities there. Negativism, sensationalism, arrogance, invasion of privacy, fictionalizing, biasing, hiding sources, class-racial-gender prejudice, misleading headlines, quoting out of context, erroneous identification, distortion, sexual and violent emphasis — on and on go the indictments of the media.

Again, as was stated earlier, the basic problem that stands behind the ethical miasma in America is the media's emphasis on freedom. And with freedom the media pay homage to individualism and have a strong aversion to government interference (Maistre). And the spirit of Machiavelli — with its emphasis on achieving one's ends, using whatever means that work — is an important part of American journalism. So the concepts of freedom and achievement are likely to push the whole area of media ethics out of the spotlight of importance.

In a discussion of ethics, the concept of freedom seems to be paramount. For many journalists freedom is more important than ethics since, they say, ethics is so subjective and relative. American political scientist Walter Berns, on the other hand, believes there is too much emphasis on freedom. In his catalytic *Freedom, Virtue, and the First Amendment*, Berns sounds the call to Aristotelian public virtue, even (like Plato) favoring censorship at times. Prurient and pornographic publications, for example, should be censored. Reflecting the thought of Aristotle, he is more concerned with virtue, good character and harmonious society than he is with freedom.

In conclusion, what is the answer to the essential twin problems of the public media — mission and ethics? One is tempted to say that the media's mission ought to be a serious concern for ethics. But with the concept of freedom being so important, perhaps there can be no answer. Mission seems to remain whatever media units want to do, and ethics is conceived as the actions that free media want to take.

If this is true, then we must resign ourselves to live in a media world of various "truths," puzzling concepts and myths, uncertain mission and unresolved ethical problems. Of course, there is the possibility that this can change, unappealing as it is: a further siphoning off of press freedom, and mission and ethics becoming determined by a paternalistic government.

But there is another possibility, however unsuccessful history has shown it to be. It is that individual journalists will of their own accord, or pressured by their communitarian allies, forge a dedicated and committed league of ethicists and freedom-fighters embracing a combination of freedom and responsibility, wisdom and virtue, that can withstand the constant threat of authoritarianism and Machiavellianism.

POSTSCRIPT

This essay has run off in many directions. It has, to a considerable degree, ignored the important rhetorical principle of unity (and perhaps, coherence) and has tried to deal with what I think are the critical issues in today's journalism. Focus, however, has been on the diversity of the media, the mission of the media, the freedom of the media and the morality of the media.

It has been a fascinating exercise for me, for I have been able to reconstruct various positions I have taken in the past, to present some new ones, and to stress others that I think are important for the journalist and the citizen alike.

Although I consider myself a libertarian, I have come to recognize the inherent danger to a society resting mainly on a free press. I agree with James Fitzjames Stephen's famous rebuttal to John Stuart Mill's *On Liberty*, in which he compared freedom of expression to fire — good and helpful in some cases and extremely destructive in others. Freedom as an abstract concept is all right, but the problem arises with those who use it. I have little patience with socially harmful media and messages and would like to see them disappear. But the specter of censorship looms up and I am forced to retreat into my earlier libertarianism. Of course, self-control and self-regulation form the rational stance, and that is why I put increasing stress on ethics. But I realize that such a utopian solution is probably unrealizable. So I still wade about in the slushy quagmire of media morality.

It is possible, however, that there is an answer. And that is to truly professionalize journalism. Numerous problems, of course, face such action. One of the main ones is how to get a profession started. Who would decide who would be in the profession? What about those journalists who would practice without being in the profession? Innumerable other such questions could be considered. But making journalism a profession would, I think, result in higher and more consistent quality, in minimum entrance requirements, common expectations, meritocratic advancement, increased loyalty, acceptance of a professional ethical code, and peer-policing, and some kind of licensing (by the profession).

At present there are no entrance requirements for journalists. Evidently there is no preferable education for journalists since anyone can be a journalist. There is no discrete body of knowledge for journalists. There is no way to get rid of anti-social, evil or unethical journalists — no way to "de-press" them. Quite simply, journalism is at present not a profession. Becoming one might improve the situation, although the public does not seem to think that being a profession helps a vocation like law very much.

With the advent of postmodernism and critical theory in the early 1950s, many of my early 20th century ideas have changed — or at least been challenged. For example, the whole matter of journalistic objectivity has been shattered (of course many of us questioned this long before postmodernists came along). Journalists are now being attacked rather routinely for not understanding that facts are simply social constructions (Richards), and therefore any so-called "objective" story is simply the journalist's perspective or viewpoint. However, I think journalists have always understood this "social construction" business, for it is not a very profound observation.

I have engaged in some of this impossibility-of-truth talk myself, even while realizing the likelihood of being misunderstood. I recall that I always encouraged the persistent pursuit of truth: the "will" to be truthful, to communicate as much of the truth as possible. The truth with a capital "T" — the Transcendental Truth — of course, we will never know. Even the most prominent theologians and philosophers have no knowledge of what that is. But some of big-T truth falls into the potential level of reality where we can get at it. The dedicated journalist, then, selects as much of this potential truth as possible for the report. And from this selected truth, the story is written or produced. Of course it is not "truthful" in the sense of matching reality, just as a map does not match the territory it depicts. But there are better and worse map-makers and there are better and worse reporters.

An interesting point is made by Australian journalism scholar Ian Richards (2005). He points out that if there is no truth, there is no untruth either, meaning that all views are equally valid. (It could be that if there is no truth, everything is untruth, but there are degrees of untruth.) One might wonder if truth and untruth are really opposites and mutually exclusive; nevertheless, it is an interesting notion. Richards says that there is also a philosophical objection to the postmodern criticism — that when such criticism asserts that there is no truth, it would mean that the assertion is not true. Score one for truth!

Morality is closely tied to mission. That is, if one accepts a relativistic view of morality. Relativism and its cousin, subjectivity, appear to be growing in popularity. A public communication medium, a certain newspaper for instance, in a certain society, has at the core of its mission the idea of news-presentation. Its moral character (if a medium can have character) is therefore predicated on the forthrightness and seriousness with which it treats news. It defines itself as "a news medium" and strives mightily to fulfill its mission of providing news. Its moral essence is composed of accurate, meaningful, balanced, unbiased, reliable information. It may, on occasion, act unethically, but it is still a moral medium. A moral person or medium, with a basically sound and respected reputation, can perform unethical acts now and then and still be moral.

What if another medium's mission is to provide entertainment, or to publicize scandal and gossip, or to make huge profits, to push an ideology or a party, or to draw people to a religion? The relativist can make the point that in each case the medium is moral if it generally does a good job at what it does. This, of course, seems nonsense to me, for I do not see morality as simply accomplishing someone's purpose, but in virtuous, humanistic motivations and activities. However, since a particular mission can affect morality positively or negatively, I suppose one might say that morality is tied to mission.

Moderation in journalism is an important concept dealt with earlier as part of the discussion of the dialectic. Of course, in a free press excess or extremism is permissible, but from a philosophical perspective the Golden Mean or the dialectical synthesis is to be sought. And even from a practical standpoint it is a wise stance, for it will attract audience members from both extremes and also from the middle.

Myths in journalism can, and do, lead to misunderstanding. They also lead to unnecessary controversies. But, by and large, they are harmless. So what if there is no realistic "right to know"? So what does that really matter? The media know that the people will know mainly what they want them to know. That is the operative point in any media system, across the spectrum from authoritarian to libertarian.

After over a half century of trying to teach journalistic practice, theory and morality, I cannot see much improvement except in the areas of technology. Writing, except in spots, has not improved; in fact, it is worse than ever. Emphasis on news is waning and popularization of media content is booming. Editing and fact-checking appear to be getting worse. Ever larger profits are sought by the media. Editorial stress on ways to improve our democratic system is generally lacking. Increasingly unethical practices are demeaning journalism, even in highly respected media.

Internet users and bloggers of all types are invading the realm of journalism, as we discussed earlier. This may well lead to a great diversity of messages available to the citizens, but it does not portend any improvement in quality or credibility. Message pluralism in our society is considered a positive thing. But is diversity without credibility necessarily a good thing? I had rather have one bit of news that I can be sure is true than to have a plethora of messages that are problematic and unverifiable. It may be that journalism will one day turn to bloggerism and everybody will be covered by the First

Amendment. I hope not, although the communitarians would likely revel in the resultant democratization of communication.

The institutionalized media may be in the process of disappearing. Morality may be adapting to various cultures and governmental systems. Public communication's mission may be splintered into a million pieces. The concept of freedom of expression may be increasingly seen as endangering society. Machiavellian pragmatism may be taking over media tactics. Postmodernism may succeed in demolishing the concept of truth and objectivity. All of this is certainly possible in the 21st century and beyond.

In conclusion, I am not optimistic about the communications media. This feeling of Schaden, that clings to me even on my best days, comes not only from the growth of the crass media and the lowering tastes of the mass media, but from the general health of our whole social-governmental system. The main Enlightenment rationale for a free press — to make for wiser citizen-rulers — is being blown away by the raging storms of egocentric extremists — left and right — who demand freedom simply for freedom's sake. And these storms are likely to sweep humanistic and inspiring messages down the dark caverns of irrationalism and emotion into a vast pit of nihilism where mission and morality are no more.

But I am no fatalist. I believe in the resilience of the human spirit and in the possibility of a society to regenerate, and in reasonable people to slow down or stop creeping societal entropy. And with such regeneration I have no doubt that public communication will resurrect itself from the swamp of vulgarization and superficiality and serve as the stimulus for the rise of a truly new world communication order.

And as for morality, the most difficult of these subjects with which to deal, let me say that after years of reading, listening to, and thinking about morality and ethics, I have come to a definition for — or conclusion about — morality. And it is a simple one: that morality stems from habitual "good-willing," to paraphrase Kant again. A strong motivation, a deep inclination to do the right thing, a spirit of humanistic concern — that is what morality is. Journalists can have it. Media can have it. Caring for others, yes, but caring also for self. When one respects self and others, he or she is moral. And the actions that come about due to this attitude of concern for the welfare of self and others are ethical actions.

A deep caring about self and personal virtue and sensitivity to the welfare of others: this is the basic humanistic moral stance. It springs from the kind of universal agape love taught by many religious leaders. It forms the solid core of morality from which all other virtues emanate. When a person or medium forsakes moral motivation, a kind of nihilistic and irresponsible existence follows. A synthesis of Aristotelian virtues and Kantian duty produces a morality that will bring a rebirth of responsible public communication and will, at the same time, provide a basic clue to the proper mission of the media.

REFERENCES

Augustine, St. 1961. *Confessions.* Baltimore: Penguin Books.

Bagdikian, Ben. 1997. *The Media Monopoly.* Boston: Beacon Press.

Barron, Jerome. 1973. *Freedom of the Press: For Whom?* Bloomington: University of Indiana Press.

Barrett, William. 1958. *Irrational Man: A Study in Existential Philosophy.* Garden City, NY: Doubleday Anchor Books.

Berlin, Isaiah. 1977. *Four Essays on Liberty.* London: Oxford University Press.

Berns, Walter. 1957. *Freedom, Virtue, and the First Amendment.* Baron Rouge: Louisiana State University Press.

Bertrand, Claude-Jean, ed. 2003. *An Arsenal for Democracy.* Cresshill, NJ: Hampton.

Carey, James W. 1989. *Communication as Culture.* Boston: Unwin-Hyman .

Chafee, Zachariah. 1947. *Government and Mass Communication.* Chicago: University of Chicago Press.

Christians, Clifford, et al. 1993. *Good News: Social Ethics and the Press.* New York: Oxford University Press.

Commission on Freedom of the Press. 1947. *A Free and Responsible Press.* Chicago: University of Chicago Press.

Confucius. *The Analects.* Many editions.

Craig, David A. 2003. "The Promise and Peril of Anecdotes in News Coverage: An Ethical Analysis," *Journalism and Mass Communication Quarterly*, 30(4), 2003.

Cunningham, Brent. Nov./Dec. 2005. *Columbia Journalism Review* (New York)

Cooper, Thomas, et al. 1989. *Communication Ethics and Global Change*. New York: Longman.

Dewey, John. 1927. *The Public and Its Problems*. New York: Henry Holt.

Dewey, John. 1963. *Liberalism and Social Action*. New York: Capricorn.

Elliott, Deni. 1988. "All is Not Relative: Essential Shared Values of the Press," *Journal of Mass Media Ethics,* 3(1) 29.

Epstein, Joseph. Jan., 2006. "Are Newspapers Doomed?" Commentary.

Etzioni, Amitai. 1993. *The Spirit of Community*. New York: Crown Publishers.

Etzioni, Amitai. 1996. *The New Golden Rule*. New York: Basic Books.

Fromm, Erich. 1941. *Escape from Freedom*. New York: Rinehart.

Fromm, Erich. 1966. *Man for Himself.* New York: New York: Fawcett Premier.

Fukuyama, F. 1999, May. "The great disruption: Human nature and the reconstitution of social order," *The Atlantic Monthly*, pp. 55-60.

Gamble, Adam & Takesato Watanabe. 2004. *A Public Betrayed: An Inside Look at Japanese Media Atrocities and Their Warnings to the West*. Washington, D.C.: Regnery Publishing, Inc.

Glasser, Theodore. 1999. *The Idea of Public Journalism*. New York: Guilford Press.

Habermas, Juergen. 1991. *Critic in the Public Sphere*. London: Routledge.

Hachten, William. 1987. *The World News Prism*. Ames: Iowa State University Press.

Hardt, Hanno. 2004. *Myths for the Masses: An Essay on Mass Communication*. Ames, Iowa: Blackwell Publishing Co.

Hayakawa, S.I. 1990. *Language in Thought and Action*. New York: Harcourt Brace Jananovich.

Hayek, Friedrich A. 1944. *The Road to Serfdom.* Chicago: Univerity of Chicago Press.

Humboldt, Wilhelm von. 1993. *On the Limits of State Action.* Indianapolis: Liberty Fund.

Hutchins, Robert. (see Commission on Freedom of the Press)

Jaspers, Karl. 1957. *Man in the Modern Age.* Garden City, NY: Doubleday.

Kant, Immanuel. 1964. *Groundwork of the Metaphysic of Morality.* New York: Harper & Row.

Kant, Immanuel. 1998. *Critique of Practical Reason.* Milwaukee: Marquette University Press.

Kierkegaard, Soren. 1968. *Fear and Trembling.* Princeton: Princeton University Press.

Korzybski, Alfred. 1933. *Science and Sanity.* Lakeville, Conn.

Kunczik, Michael, ed. 1999. *Ethics in Journalism: A Reader on their perception in the Third World.* Bonn: Friedrich Ebert-Stiftung.

Kupperman, Joel. 1999. *Learning from Asian Philosophy.* Oxford: Oxford University Press.

Lambeth, Edmund. 1986. *Committed Journalism.* Bloomington: Indiana University Press.

Land, Mitchell, and Bill Hornaday. 2006. *Contemporary Media Ethics.* Spokane, WA: Marquette Books.

Leslie, Larry Z. 2004. *Mass Communication Ethics: Decision Making in Postmodern Culture.* Boston: Houghton Mifflin Company.

Lewis, C. S. 2001. *Mere Christianity.* San Francisco: Harper.

Lippmann, Walter. 1922. *Public Opinion.* New York: Free Press.

Locke, John. 1993. *Of Civil Government.* New York: E.P. Dutton and Co.

Machiavelli, Niccolo. *The Prince.* Many editions.

Marx, Karl. 1932. *Capital, The Communist Manifesto, and Other Writings.* New York: The Modern Library.

McChesney, Robert. 1997. *Corporate Media and the Threat to Democracy.* New York: Seven Stories Press.

McChesney, Robert. 1999. *Rich Media, Poor Democracy.* Urbana: U. of Illinois Press.

McCombs, Max. 1997. *Communication and Democracy*. Mahwah, NJ: Lawrence Erlbaum Associates.

McLuhan, Marshall. 1965. *Understanding Media*. New York: McGraw-Hill.

Merrill, John C. 1968. *The Elite Press: Great Newspapers of the World*. New York: Pitman Publishing Co.

Merrill, John C. 1974. *The Imperative of Freedom: A Philosophy of Journalistic Autonomy*. New York: Hastings House.

Merrill, John C. 1989. *The Dialectic in Journalism: Toward a Responsible Use of Press Freedom*. Baton Rouge: LSU Press.

Merrill, John C. 1996. *Existential Journalism*. Ames: Iowa State University Press.

Merrill, J.C., R. Berenger, and C. Merrill, 2003. *Media Musings: Interviews with Great Thinkers*. Spokane, WA: Marquette Books.

Mill, John Stuart. 1986. *On Liberty*. New York: Macmillan.

Niebuhr, Reinhold. 1957. (Introduction). *Responsibility in Mass Communication*, by Wilbur Schramm. New York: Harper & Brothers.

Nietzsche, Friedrich. 1966. *Beyond Good and Evil*. New York: Random House.

Noelle-Neumann, Elisabeth. 1983. *The Spiral of Silence*. Chicago: University of Chicago Press.

Palser, Barb. 2005, Aug/Sept. *American Journalism Review*, pp. 43-50.

Plato. 1974. *Plato's Republic*. Indianapolis: Hackett. (Trans. G.M.A. Grude).

Popper, Karl R. 1930. *The Open Society and Its Enemies*. Princeton: University Press.

Porter, Burton P. 1995. *The Good Life: Alternatives in Ethics*. New York: Ardsley.

Posner, Richard. 2005, July 31. "Bad News," *The New York Times*.

Rand, Ayn. 1961. *For the New Intellectual*. New York: Signet Books.

Rawls, John. 1971. *Theory of Justice*. Cambridge: Harvard University Press.

Richards, Ian. 2005. *Quagmires and Quandaries: Exploring Journalism Ethics.* Sydney, Australia: University of New South Wales.

Rosen, Jay. 1996. *Getting the Connections Right: Public Journalism and the Troubles in the Press.* New York: Twentieth Century Fund.

Russell, Bertrand. 1962, *Human Society in Ethics and Politics.* New York: Mentor.

Saint Augustine. 1943. *The Confessions of St. Augustine.* New York: Citadel Press.

Sartre, Jean-Paul. 1957. *Existentialism and Human Emotions.* New York: Philosophical Library.

Seidenberg, R. 1974. *Posthistoric Man.* New York: Viking Press.

Siebert, F., T. Peterson, and W. Schramm. 1963. *Four Theories of the Press.* Urbana: University of Illinois Press.

Snow, C.P. 1959. *The Two Cultures.* (The Rede Lecture). Cambridge: University Press.

Spencer, Herbert. 1887. *The Factors of Organic Evolution.* London: Williams and Norgate.

Spencer, Herbert. 1884. *The Man 'versus' the State.* London: Williams and Norgate. .

Thorson, Thomas L., (ed.) 1963. *Plato: Totalitarian or Democrat?* Englewood Cliffs, NJ: Prentice-Hall.

Tocqueville, Alexis de. 1966. *Democracy in America.* New York: Harper & Row. (Original work published 1838).

Walbridge, John. 2000. *The Leaven of the Ancients: Suhrawardi and the Heritage of The Greeks.* Albany: State Univer.of New York Press.

Weaver, Richard. 1948. *Ideas Have Consequences.* Chicago: Univ. of Chicago Press.

Wiener, Norbert. 1950. *The Human Use of Human Beings.* Boston: Houghton-Mifflin.

Wilson, E.O. 1998 (March). "Back from Chaos," *The Atlantic Monthly.*

Wittgenstein, Ludwig. 1922. *Tractatus Logico-Philosophicus.* London: Routledge and Kegan Paul.

Zakaria, Fareed. 2003. *The Future of Freedom: Illiberal Democracy at Home and Abroad.* New York: W.W. Norton & Company.

Zinn, Howard. 1980. *The People's History of the United States.* New York: Harper & Row.

INDEX

A

accountability system, 59
age of the Internet, 25
Age of Reason, 10, 26, 78, 104
American Journalism Review, 66, 118
Aristotle, 11, 70, 72, 74, 76, 77, 98, 99, 101, 106
Atlanta Constitution, 44
attitudinal illiterates, 46
Augustine, St., 11, 19, 119

B

Bagdikian, Ben, 53, 105
Barron, Jerome, 52
Benedict, Ruth, 37
Berkeley, Bishop, 28, 43
Berlin, Isaiah, 70
Berns, Walter, 106
Bertrand, Claude-Jean, 59
Bill of Rights, 51
Black, Jay, 11
bloggers, 2, 7, 10, 58, 66-68, 111
Bradlee, Ben, 105
Buddhism, 93

Burke, Edmund, 53, 70

C

D

E

I

idealism, 82

J

Jaspers, Karl, 103
Jefferson, Thomas, 40
journalistic philosophers, 39

K

Kant, Immanuel, 76, 90, 96
Koppel, Ted, 43
Korzybski, Alfred, 26
Kovach, Bill, 104

L

Landrieu, Mary, 27
Le Monde, 43
Lewis, C. S., 99
Lippmann, Walter, 94
Locke, John, 52, 60, 75

M

Machiavelli, 11, 91, 106, 117
Man for Himself, 26, 116
mass media, 4, 10, 11, 13, 44-47, 82, 83, 90, 93, 104, 105, 112, 116
McChesney, Robert, 19, 61
McLuhan, Marshall, 13
media bias, 70
media-audience pyramid, 42
Meyer, Frank, 33
Meyer, Phil, 11

Milwaukee Journal, 45
Montesquieu, 70
morality, 1, 3, 7, 11, 13, 14, 69, 75, 83, 89-92, 95, 96, 98, 108-113, 117
Moyers, Bill, 19
Murdoch, Iris, 101

N

National Public Radio (NPR), 43, 105
National Geographic, 43
National Review, 43
naturalistic fallacy, 102
Neue Zuercher Zeitung, 43
New Republic, 43
New York Times, The, 28, 43, 45, 67, 90, 105, 118
news, 2, 7, 13, 15-18, 20, 21, 23-25, 27-32, 35, 37, 38, 43-46, 50, 52-57, 64, 66, 68, 71, 77, 80-82, 84, 85, 89, 90, 104, 110, 111, 115, 116, 118
Nietzsche, Friedrich, 33, 73
Noelle-Neumann, Elisabeth, 11, 34, 118
normative ethics, 11
noumena, 49

O

objectivity, 20, 23, 26-28, 30, 73, 74, 92, 109, 112
On Liberty, 108, 115, 118
Oriental thinkers, 99
Orlando Sentinel, 44

P

Palser, Barb, 66
paradox of freedom, 60
PBS, 43

People magazine, 15
people's right to know, 51
Pew Foundation, 61
Philosopher king, 40, 61
Plato, 11, 19, 39, 47, 60, 63, 64, 74, 77, 85, 100, 103, 106, 118, 119
Plato's Cave, 27
pluralism of media, 56
Popper, Karl, 60, 77, 92
postmodernism, 10, 20, 26, 52, 71, 74, 109, 112
press freedom, 37, 58-60, 62, 63, 80, 94, 106, 118
propaganda, 13, 16, 21-23, 25, 54, 77, 94, 104
public journalism, 21, 41, 61, 62, 116, 119
Public Broadcasting System (PBS), 43

Q

Quill magazine, 51

R

Rand, Ayn, 53, 101
Republic (Plato's), 39, 42, 43, 58, 74, 103, 118
Richards, Ian, 92, 110
right to know, 51, 84, 97, 111
Road to Serfdom, 54, 117
Rousseau, Jean Jacques, 69, 101
Russell, Bertrand, 102

S

Schadenfreude, 23
Schoenbach, Klaus, 11
Schramm, Wilbur, 11, 118
Seidenberg, Roderick, 64
Shreveport Times, 44

T

U

V

W

Weaver, Richard, 47
Weber, Max, 97
Wiener, Norbert, 12
Wilkins, Lee, 89

Z

Zinn, Howard, 61